Judicial Minimalism – For and Against
Edited by Yasutomo Morigiwa and Hirohide Takikawa

ARCHIV FÜR RECHTS- UND SOZIALPHILOSOPHIE

ARCHIVES FOR PHILOSOPHY OF LAW AND SOCIAL PHILOSOPHY

ARCHIVES DE PHILOSOPHIE DU DROIT ET DE PHILOSOPHIE SOCIALE

ARCHIVO DE FILOSOFÍA JURÍDICA Y SOCIAL

Herausgegeben von der Internationalen Vereinigung

für Rechts- und Sozialphilosophie (IVR)

Redaktion: Dr. Annette Brockmöller, LL. M.

Beiheft 132

Judicial Minimalism – For and Against

Proceedings of the 9th Kobe Lectures. Tokyo, Nagoya, and Kyoto, June 2008

Edited by Yasutomo Morigiwa and Hirohide Takikawa

Franz Steiner Verlag

Nomos

Bibliografische Information der Deutschen Nationalbibliothek:
Die Deutsche Nationalbibliothek verzeichnet diese Publikation in der Deutschen Nationalbibliografie; detaillierte bibliografische Daten sind im Internet über <http://dnb.d-nb.de> abrufbar.

Druck: Druckhaus Nomos, Sinzheim
Gedruckt auf säurefreiem, alterungsbeständigem Papier.
Printed in Germany.
Franz Steiner Verlag: ISBN 978-3-515-10136-3
Nomos Verlag: ISBN 978-3-8487-0013-4

Table of Contents

MORIGIWA Yasutomo

Sunstein on Judicial Minimalism

It is with great pleasure that my fellow editor and I present the proceedings of the Ninth Kobe Lecture. This is on behalf of the Japanese National Section of the International Association for Philosophy of Law and Social Philosophy (IVR Japan) and the Japan Association of Legal Philosophy (JALP)[1]. The invited lecturer, Professor Cass R. SUNSTEIN[2], read his Kobe Lecture "Beyond Judicial Minimalism" in Kyoto, at the University of Kyoto.[3] Seminars were also given in Tokyo and Nagoya, where in-depth discussion took place, especially between the designated commentators and Professor SUNSTEIN. So much so, in fact, that instead of the usual format of the Kobe Lecture, which is the publication of the lecture in a regular issue of the *Archiv fuer Rechts- und Sozialphilosophie* (*ARSP*, the official publishing organ of the IVR[4]), a project was developed to publish the lecture, commentaries and the lecturer's reply to the commentators in a single volume. With the kind understanding of the managing editor of the *ARSP*, the project became reality in the form of the *Beiheft* you see here, entitled *Beyond Judicial Minimalism: for and against*.

In his Lecture, Cass SUNSTEIN reflects upon his Judicial Minimalism, a doctrine asserting that the proper role of the judiciary is to go "narrow and shallow," collectively making minimal changes to its jurisprudence. He goes "beyond Judicial Minimalism" by reflecting on the goal and conditions that make the minimalist strategy reasonable, culminating in the conclusion that there are situations when a different strategy is more efficient.

A precise and comprehensive analysis of the character and system of SUNSTEIN's thought is available in the commentary by my co-editor, TAKIKAWA Hirohide (Rikkyo). SUNSTEIN himself, in replying to TAKIKAWA at the Nagoya seminar, remarked that the commentator knew more about his theory than himself. I therefore take the liberty of discussing SUNSTEIN's views from my own, perhaps myopic point of view.

Judicial Minimalism is an ingenious way of understanding what judges are really doing, especially in judicial review. Traditional "theories" of legal interpreta-

1 http://www.houtetsugaku.org/en/index.html
2 The Felix Frankfurter Professor of Law at Harvard Law School. Now on leave to serve in the Obama Administration as the Administrator of the White House Office of Information and Regulatory Affairs.
3 Co-sponsored by the Program funded by Grant-in-Aid for Creative Scientific Research "Law and Ordering of Market and Society in the Post -'Structural Reform'Era: A New Legal System for Liberty and Communality" at the School of Law, the University of Kyoto.
4 Internationale Vereinigung fuer Rechts- und Sozialphilosophie, or the International Association for Philosophy of Law and Social Philosophy, founded 1909.

tion prove to be of little use here, as in other contexts. The issue for the judge is to give a satisfactory solution to the case at hand, a solution which can provide *de facto* if not normative guidance to future decisions, both by the judiciary and the public. What is the criteria that such a judicial decision should satisfy? A decent judicial decision must simultaneously provide society, seemingly two incompatible functions of the law, namely, authority and justice. I.e., on the one hand, to provide security and stability to the system of law by keeping the role that law plays in society constant; on the other, to produce and maintain justice through law, by keeping the legal system in tune with the times and the legal decision appropriate to the case at hand. Less able theorists than SUNSTEIN have referred to this as the problem of "balancing stability through law with justice in the concrete case." Judicial Minimalism may be understood as a name for the strategy by which such a seemingly impossible task is realized.

SUNSTEIN goes beyond judicial minimalism by treading beyond the scope of the judicial system and examines the role of the judiciary within the system of separation of powers: its proper role in a democratic government and a liberal society. It is the responsibility of the legislature to come up with major policy decisions; the judiciary is to avoid taking on such a role if it can be avoided. Legal reasoning is not tailored for this type of political decision-making. Decision making in the judiciary is a piecemeal process, not a revolutionary one. However, it should be noted that though piecemeal, the result of collective path-blazing and treading may sometimes culminate in a revolutionary view on what justice requires. I consider SUNSTEIN's theory, which leads to the development of this way of understanding law, a significant step in the advancement of legal philosophy.

There is one aspect, however, in which the editors do not see quite eye to eye with Cass SUNSTEIN. In replying to the commentators in his "On Fallibility: A Reply," SUNSTEIN stresses the importance of the acknowledgement of human fallibility and bounded rationality in general. If we pay due attention to this feature of the *conditio humana*, we are bound to have a certain moral attitude toward others. He thus concludes his reply:

> In both private and public life, people's fundamental convictions may seem to be at stake, and one or another approach might repudiate the defining beliefs of one or another group. In some cases, judges and others are explicitly asked to take sides. Of course it is true that in prominent cases, it is crucial to take sides .... But in many cases, reasonable people differ, and in such cases, it is important for human beings, including judges, to acknowledge their own fallibility. One of America's greatest judges, Learned Hand, once said that "the spirit of liberty is that spirit which is not too sure that it is right." An acknowledgement of fallibility, central to minimalism, is a way of respecting liberty's spirit; and it carries with it a strong signal of mutual respect.

As to this view of mutual respect, I agree with TAKIKAWA, who points out:

> However, the point here is the quality of respect. Mutual respect in incompletely theorized agreements implies that we should not challenge our "fellow citizen's deepest and most defining commitments."[5] This kind of respect is superficial. Since we are not required to give them reasons for our conclusions, we do not treat them as rational agents. We defer to their strong convictions because they blindly devote themselves to their fallacious beliefs. We tolerate them because they are pitiful. … We fail to show reasonable respect to each other unless we try to grant justificatory reasons for our actions and decisions, even if we often disagree about what they really are.

The Kobe Lecture is an international lecture program founded in 1988, commemorating the Thirteenth World Congress on Philosophy of Law and Social Philosophy held in August 1997 in Kobe, Japan. The lectures are administered by IVR Japan, in cooperation with JALP. As a rule, every two years (three, since 2002), a scholar engaged in creative research of basic issues of legal, social and political philosophy is invited to Japan. The lecturer usually gives one or two lectures in major cities of Japan in addition to several informal seminars. Major works by the lecturer are usually translated into Japanese and published before the lectures take place.

Professor Ronald DWORKIN (New York) gave the Inaugural Lecture in 1990. Professor Ralf DREIER was the second lecturer in 1992. In 1994, Professor Joseph RAZ (Columbia) gave the third series of Lectures. The Fourth Lecture was extraordinary in that it was given in the form of the First Asia Symposium in Jurisprudence, the first international conference to be held under the program. The theme for the symposium, held in October 1996, was "Law in a Changing World: Asian alternatives." Professor Will KYMLICKA (Queens, Canada) gave the Fifth Lecture in 1998. The Sixth was given in the year 2000 by Professor Randy BARNETT (Georgetown). In 2002, Professor Emilios CHRISTODOULIDIS (Glasgow) gave the Seventh Lecture. IVR Japan and JALP decided to hold the Kobe Lectures every three years instead of two hereon in. The Eighth Lecture was given in the year 2005 by Professor Ulfrid NEUMANN (Frankfurt). Professor Cass SUNSTEIN (Chicago, then) gave the Ninth in 2008. The lectures are published in the *ARSP*. The proceedings of the Fourth and the Fifth Lectures are published as a special issue (Beihefte 72 and 96, respectively) of the journal, as is this Lecture.

The Kobe Lecture aims to advance our understanding of legal, social and the political spheres of life. Important theoretical issues are explored from a perspective that is philosophical yet sensitive to problems of implementation and administration. Through this program we hope to arrive at a deeper mutual understanding of both the similarities and differences among various cultures.

The editors wish to thank Cass SUNSTEIN for his willingness to reply to the commentators and for his patience and cooperation in preparing the publication. We would also like to express our appreciation to the commentators for insights Professor SUNSTEIN himself must have enjoyed. It is a pleasure to express our gratitude once again (*vide* Beihefte 72 and 96) to Prof. Veronica TAYLOR, whose

5 Sunstein (note 2), 12.

team has come through yet again to do a great job of editing for grammar, style and effect the papers written by our Japanese colleagues.

For the Ninth Lecture, the editors were themselves heavily involved in its organization. MORIGIWA Yasutomo (Nagoya), the then acting president of IVR, served as the chair of the organizing committee as well as the manager and translator of the Nagoya seminar, and TAKIKAWA Hirohide, was the most active member of the committee as well as being a brilliant contributor. The editors would like to thank KAWAMI Makoto (Aoyama Gakuin Women's Junior College), for managing the Tokyo lecture and seminars, and HATTORI Takahiro (Kyoto), representing the project funded by Grant-in-Aid for Creative Scientific Research "Law and Ordering of Market and Society in the Post -'Structural Reform' Era: A New Legal System for Liberty and Communality" for co-sponsoring the Kobe Lecture, held at Kyoto University.

We would also like to express our deep gratitude for all those who had contributed their time and effort, working with the organizers to make this Lecture as fruitful as it has turned out to be. The editors express their appreciation to the then President SHIMAZU Itaru and the executive board of JALP for their unflinching support of the program. On behalf of the contributors to this volume, as well as JALP and IVR Japan, we wish to express our appreciation to the managing editor of *ARSP*, Richterlin am Bundesgerichtshof Dr. Annette BROCKMOELLER, for accepting our proposal. Thanks are also due to Ms. Sarah SCHÄFER of Franz Steiner Verlag for her ever quick and positive response and help in the publication process.

The Ninth Kobe Lecture

Cass R. Sunstein,* Harvard University, Cambridge, USA

Beyond Judicial Minimalism

Abstract

Many judges are minimalists. They favor rulings that are narrow, in the sense that they govern only the circumstances of the particular case, and also shallow, in the sense that they do not accept a deep theory of the legal provision at issue. In law, narrow and shallow decisions have real advantages insofar as they reduce both decision costs and error costs; make space for democratic engagement on fundamental questions; and reflect a norm of civic respect. In many cases, however, minimalism is hard to justify in these ways. Sometimes small steps increase the aggregate costs of decisions; sometimes they produce large errors, especially when they export decision-making burdens to fallible people. Predictability is an important variable, and minimalist decisions can compromise predictability. Sometimes large, non-minimalist steps serve democratic values and do not compromise the norm of civic respect. It follows that the justifications for minimalism are unconvincing in many contexts. The debate between minimalists and their adversaries is closely related to the debate between those who prefer standards and those who prefer rules, though there are some important differences.

I. The Argument[1]

Many judges prefer to avoid broad rulings and theoretical ambition. My goal here is to attempt to understand the justifications for this preference and to explore their limitations. As we shall see, avoidance and modest ambition have an important place in law. But in some domains, minimalism is a terrible blunder.

To offer a preview of my central claims: Many of the arguments on behalf of minimalism are essentially pragmatic. For example, minimalists care the costs of decision and the costs of error. Minimalists believe that their approach will minimize both of these costs. Minimalists also point to the importance of democratic self-government and a norm of civic respect. Minimalists believe that by leaving central issues undecided, they can maintain ample space for self-governance while also demonstrating respect to people who disagree on fundamental matters.

* Felix Frankfurter Professor of Law, Harvard Law School. An earlier version of this essay was delivered as the Kobe Lecture in Japan in July 2008; I am most grateful to my hosts for their kindness and substantive suggestions on that occasion. Readers are asked to make allowances for an essay originally intended for oral delivery.

1 I have dealt with aspects of this problem in other places, and I draw on some of the treatments there. See Cass R. Sunstein, One Case At A Time, 1999; Legal Reasoning and Political Conflict, 1996. The distinctive feature of this essay consists in the effort to describe the limits of mimimalism and to specify the circumstances in which judges should go beyond it.

In many contexts, however, these arguments fail to provide an adequate defense of minimalism. Sometimes minimalist rulings increase the costs of decisions and the costs of errors. If courts take small steps, they will impose serious burdens on others, and if future decisionmakers (lower courts, administrative agencies) are unreliable, minimalism might produce many mistakes. Predictability is an important value, and minimalist rulings make predictability impossible to achieve. Non-minimalist rulings can increase democratic space, certainly insofar as they give an authoritative signal that elected officials are permitted to do as they want. By contrast, minimalist decisions require officials to speculate about what the Court will ultimately do. Civic respect is unquestionably important, but sometimes the Constitution is properly read to declare certain practices off-limits. In law, as in ordinary life, the justifications for minimalism frequently fail, and hence sensible judges sometimes find it necessary to go beyond minimalism.

II. Minimalisms

A. Shallow and Narrow

When people are confronted with a difficult decision, they often move in the direction of minimalism. Minimalists prefer modest steps over ambitious ones. This preference operates along two distinct dimensions.

First, minimalists want to proceed in a way that is *shallow rather than deep*. In deciding what to do with a relationship or a medical problem, minimalists want to leave the foundational issues undecided. They want to decide what to do, today or tomorrow or next month, without resolving the deepest questions, or without accepting some large account of how the relationship or the problem should be handled.

Second, minimalists want to proceed in way that is *narrow rather than wide*. They want to decide what to do about next month's vacation, or a current problem in the workplace, without deciding how to handle many future vacations, or what to do about problems in the workplace in general. In ordinary life, minimalism, in the form of shallowness and narrowness, can provide a great deal of help with difficult situations. Sensible people often take small steps for that reason.

But for those who embrace minimalism, there is an evident problem. Sometimes shallowness is a bad idea; sometimes it is best to rethink foundational issues. Occasionally one needs to make a large-scale decision about a medical problem. Sometimes it is best to settle on a course of action for the workplace and even vacations, rather than to rest content with a series of small decisions. Minimalism might be easiest in the short-run, but in the long-run, it can be extremely destructive. It can be destructive in part because it exports the burdens of decision to one's future self, in a way that might produce a great deal of trouble. However difficult a large decision may be, it may be best to make it, and sooner rather than later.

To come to terms with minimalism, it is necessary to consider the costs of decisions and the costs of errors. Minimalist judgments might decrease those costs, because they reduce the burdens of decisions in particular cases, and because in some circumstances, they reduce the number and magnitude of errors as well. If people lack information that would justify confidence in width, narrowness might be much better. Shallowness might have virtues for the same reason. But we can easily imagine situations in which both depth and width are preferable. A series of case-by-case decisions, with respect to the workplace or a course of medical treatment, might increase the burdens of decision on balance. In addition, such decisions might increase rather than decrease errors. Sometimes people take large steps, rather than small ones, as a way of simplifying their decision-making burdens and ensuring that overall errors will be reduced.

In law, minimalism plays an exceedingly important role. Some judges favor shallow rulings. Such rulings attempt to produce rationales and outcomes on which diverse people can agree, notwithstanding their disagreement on fundamental issues. For example, there are vigorous disputes about the underlying purpose of the free speech guarantee: Should the guarantee be seen as protecting democratic self-government, or the marketplace of ideas, or individual autonomy? Minimalists hope not to resolve these disputes. They seek judgments and rulings that can attract shared support from people who are committed to one or another of these foundational understandings, or who are unsure about the foundations of the free speech principle.

Minimalist judges also like narrow rulings, which do not venture far beyond the problem at hand. They attempt to focus on the particulars of the dispute before the Court. Consider in this light American Chief Justice John Roberts's suggestion that one advantage of unanimous decisions from the Court is that unanimity leads to narrower rulings. In his words, "[t]he broader the agreement among the justices, the more likely it is a decision on the narrowest possible grounds."[1] The nine justices have highly diverse views, and if they are able to join a single opinion, that opinion is likely to be narrow rather than broad. This, in the Chief Justice's view, is entirely desirable, as he explained with an aphoristic summary of the pro-narrowness position in constitutional law: "If it is not necessary to decide more to dispose of a case, in my view it is necessary not to decide more."

It is important to see that in many domains, including law, shallowness and narrowness are very different. We could imagine a decision that is *shallow but wide*. Consider, for example, the view that racial segregation is always forbidden, unaccompanied by any deep account of what is wrong with racial segregation. We could also imagine a decision that is *deep but narrow*. Consider, for example, a ban

1 Hon. John G. Roberts, Jr., Chief Justice, U.S. Supreme Court, Commencement Address at the Georgetown University Law Center (May 21, 2006).

on censorship of a particular political protest, accompanied by a theoretically ambitious account of the free speech principle, but limited to the particular situation in which censorship has been imposed. A decision might be both shallow and narrow or both wide and deep, but the two distinctions point in different directions.

It should be clear that both distinctions are ones of degree rather than kind. In most contexts, courts should not decide important cases without giving reasons, and reasons ensure at least some degree of depth. No one favors rulings that are limited to people with the same names or initials as those of the litigants before the Court. But among reasonable alternatives, minimalists show a persistent preference for the shallower and narrower options, especially in cases at the frontiers of constitutional law. In such cases, minimalists fear that justices lack relevant information; they do not have a full sense of the many situations to which a broad rule might apply. Minimalists also fear the potentially harmful effects of decisions that reach far beyond the case at hand. They distrust width and depth because they think that judges are often in a poor position to adopt a theoretically contentious view or to produce a wide rule.

I will return to these points, and to minimalists' characteristic timidity (cowardice?) shortly. For the moment let us notice that to defend their approach, minimalists will seek to argue that shallow, narrow rulings will minimize decision costs and error costs. By avoiding depth and width, minimalists hope to reduce decision-making burdens. Emphasizing what judges do not know, minimalists characteristically believe that theoretical depth, and width, will produce a great deal of trouble for the future. Minimalists need not speak only in these terms. They might add that if certain foundational questions are unresolved, citizens and representatives have room to debate them, in a way that is valuable for democratic reasons. Consider the scope of the Second Amendment, the power of the president over the independent regulatory commissions, the nature of executive privilege. Perhaps it is desirable that these issues remain unresolved and that participants in politics can debate the constitutional issues without a clear ruling from the Supreme Court.

As in ordinary life, however, we can imagine circumstances in which minimalism cannot be defended on the pragmatic grounds that minimalists characteristically invoke. A series of case-by-case rulings might increase the burden of decision, rather than diminishing them. And if minimalists avoid width, they might unleash subsequent decisionmakers in a way that will produce more errors overall. Uncertainty can produce serious problems for both citizens and representatives. I will return to these objections below.

B. Hollowness, Shallowness, and Conceptual Descents

It seems clear that people can often agree on constitutional *practices*, and even on constitutional rights, when they cannot agree on constitutional *theories*. In other words, well-functioning constitutional orders try to solve problems through *incompletely theorized agreements*.[2]

Sometimes these agreements involve abstractions, accepted as such amidst severe disagreements on particular cases. We might think of incompletely theorized abstractions as *hollow*, in the sense that they must be filled, and have not yet been filled, with some kind of specification. Thus people who disagree on whether the Constitution should protect incitement to violence and hate speech can accept a general free speech principle, and those who disagree about whether the Constitution should protect same-sex relationships can accept an abstract antidiscrimination principle. This is an important phenomenon in constitutional law and politics; it makes constitution-making possible. Constitution-makers can agree on abstractions without agreeing on the particular meaning of those abstractions.

A pragmatic argument on behalf of hollowness, in the form of incompletely theorized abstractions, is that nothing else is feasible. Perhaps an effort at specification will prove too contentious; citizens will support the abstraction but not the specification. Or perhaps constitution-makers lack the information that would give them reason for confidence in any specification. If so, the best way to proceed may be to set out a general norm, and to allow posterity to fill it in as it seems fit. As with small steps, hollowness may reduce the burdens of decisions while also minimizing errors. If the drafters of a constitution attempt to specify certain provisions – involving, for example, the power of the executive branch, or the precise content of an equality principle – they may blunder badly, especially when circumstances are likely to change over time.

But sometimes incompletely theorized agreements involve concrete outcomes rather than abstractions. In hard cases, people can often agree that a certain practice is or is not constitutional, even when the theories that underlie their judgments sharply diverge. In the day-to-day operation of constitutional practice, shallow rulings help to ensure a sense of what the law is, even amidst large-scale disagreements about what, particularly, accounts for those rules and doctrines.

This latter phenomenon suggests a general strategy for handling some of the most difficult decisions. In ordinary life, we might attempt to bracket the fundamental issues and decide that however they are best resolved, a particular approach makes sense for the next month or year. So too in law, politics, and morality. When people disagree or are uncertain about an abstract issue – is equality more important than liberty? does free will exist? is utilitarianism right? does pun-

2 I discuss such agreements in detail in Cass R. Sunstein, *Legal Reasoning and Political Conflict*, 1996.

ishment have retributive aims? – they can often make progress by moving to a level of greater particularity. They attempt a *conceptual descent*. This phenomenon has an especially notable feature: It enlists silence, on certain basic questions, as a device for producing convergence despite disagreement, uncertainty, limits of time and capacity, and heterogeneity. In short, silence can be a constructive force. Incompletely theorized agreements are an important source of successful constitutionalism and social stability; they also provide a way for people to demonstrate mutual respect.

Consider some examples. People may believe that it is important to protect religious liberty while having quite diverse theories about why this is so. Some people may stress what they see as the need for social peace; others may think that religious liberty reflects a principle of equality and a recognition of human dignity; others may invoke utilitarian considerations; still others may think that religious liberty is itself a theological command. Similarly, people may invoke many different grounds for their shared belief that the Constitution should ensure an independent judiciary. Some may think that judicial independence helps ensure against tyranny; others may think that it makes government more democratic; still others may think that it leads to greater efficiency in economic terms.

The agreement on particulars is incompletely theorized in the sense that the relevant participants are clear on the practice or the result without agreeing on the most general theory that accounts for it. Often people can agree that a rule – protecting political dissenters, forbidding government to take private property without paying compensation – makes sense without entirely agreeing on the foundations of their belief. They may accept an outcome – affirming the right to marry, protecting sexually explicit art, banning racial segregation – without understanding or converging on an ultimate ground for that acceptance. Often people can agree not merely on the outcome, but also on a rationale offering low-level or mid-level principles on its behalf. But what ultimately accounts for the outcome, in terms of a full-scale theory of the right or the good, is left unexplained.

There is an extreme case of incomplete theorization, offered when disagreement is especially intense: *full particularity*. This phenomenon occurs when people agree on a result without agreeing on any kind of supporting rationale. They announce what they want to do without offering a reason for doing it. Any rationale – any reason – is by definition more abstract than the result that it supports. Sometimes people do not offer reasons at all, because they do not know what those reasons are, or because they cannot agree on reasons, or because they fear that the reasons that they have would turn out, on reflection, to be inadequate and hence to be misused in the future. Here decisions are maximally shallow and maximally narrow. Juries usually do not offer reasons for outcomes, and negotiators sometimes conclude that something should happen without saying why it should happen. I will not emphasize this limiting case here, and shall focus instead on outcomes accompanied by low-level or mid-level principles.

My emphasis on shallowness in the form of incompletely theorized agreements is intended partly as descriptive. These agreements are a pervasive phenomenon in constitution-making and constitutional law. Such agreements are crucial to the effort to make effective decisions amidst intense disagreement. But I mean to make some points about constitutionalism amidst pluralism as well. In short, there are real virtues to avoiding large-scale theoretical conflicts. Incompletely theorized agreements can operate as foundations for both rules and analogies, and such agreements are especially well-suited to the limits of many diverse institutions, including legislators and courts. Incompletely theorized agreements have their place in the private sector as well. They can be found on university faculties, in the workplace, and even within families. At the same time, there are many problems with incomplete theorization, and I shall spend some of time on those problems here.

C. Converging on Practices

It seems clear that outside of law, people may agree on a *correct* outcome even though they do not have a theory to account for their judgments. You may know that dropped objects fall, that snow melts, and that hot stoves burn, without knowing exactly why these facts are true. The same is true for morality, both in general and insofar as it bears on constitutional law. You may know that slavery and genocide are wrong, that government may not stop political protests, that every person should have just one vote, and that it is bad for government to take your land unless it pays for it, without knowing exactly or entirely why these things are so. Moral judgments may be right or true even if they are reached by people who lack a full account of those judgments (though moral reasoners may well do better if they try to offer such an account, a point to which I will return). The same is true for law, constitutional and otherwise. A judge may know that if government punishes religious behavior, it has acted unlawfully, without having a full account of why this principle has been accepted as law. We may thus offer an epistemological point: People can know *that* X is true without entirely knowing *why* X is true.

Something similar holds for politics and law as well. Sometimes people can agree on individual judgments even if they disagree on general theory. In American constitutional law, for example, diverse judges may agree that *Roe v. Wade*,[3] protecting the right to choose abortion, should not be overruled, though the reasons that lead each of them to that conclusion sharply diverge. Some people think that the Court should respect its own precedents; others think that *Roe* was rightly decided as a way of protecting women's equality; others think that the case was

3 410 U.S. 113 (1973). On the refusal to overrule Roe, see Planned Parenthood v. Casey, 505 US 833 (1992).

rightly decided as a way of protecting privacy; others think that the decision reflects an appropriate judgment about the social role of religion; still others think that restrictions on abortion are unlikely to protect fetuses in the world, and so the decision is good for pragmatic or consequentialist reasons. We can find incompletely theorized political agreements on particular outcomes in many areas of law and politics – on both sides of disputes over national security, on both sides of equality controversies, both sides of disputes over criminal justice, both sides of disputes over taxation. And in some cases, the incompletely theorized agreements can obtain assent from both sides.

D. Hollowness vs. Shallowness

Incompletely theorized agreements play a pervasive role in constitutional law and in society generally. Return to agreements that are hollow in the sense that people who accept the principle need not agree on what it entails in particular cases. The agreement is hollow in the sense that it is incompletely specified. Much of the key work must be done by others, often through case-by-case judgments, specifying the hollow abstraction at the point of application. Constitutional provisions usually protect such rights as "freedom of speech," "religious liberty," and "equality under the law," and citizens agree on those abstractions in the midst of sharp dispute about what these provisions really entail. Much lawmaking also becomes possible only because of this phenomenon. And when agreement on a written constitution is difficult or impossible, it is because it is hard to obtain consensus on the governing abstractions. Consider the case of Israel, which lacks a written constitution because citizens have been unable to agree about basic principles, even if they are pitched at a high level of abstraction.

Observers of democratic constitutionalism might place particular emphasis on a different kind of phenomenon, of special interest for constitutional law in courts: incompletely theorized agreements on particular outcomes, accompanied by agreements on the shallow principles that account for them. There is no algorithm by which to distinguish between a high-level theory and one that operates at an intermediate or lower level. We might consider, as conspicuous examples of high-level theories, Kantianism and utilitarianism, and see illustrations in the many distinguished (academic) efforts to understand such areas as tort law, contract law, free speech, and the law of equality as undergirded by highly abstract theories of the right or the good. By contrast, we might think of shallow principles as including most of the ordinary material of constitutional justification or constitutional "doctrine" – the general class of principles and justifications that courts tend to offer. These principles and justifications are not said to derive from any particular large theories of the right or the good, have ambiguous relations to large theories, and are compatible with more than one such theory.

Recall that by the term "shallow principles," I refer to something relative, not absolute; I mean to do the same thing with the terms "theories" and "abstractions" (which I use interchangeably). In this setting, the notions "shallow," "high," and "abstract" are best understood in comparative terms, like the terms "big" and "old" and "unusual." Thus the "clear and present danger" standard for regulation of speech in American law is a relative abstraction when compared with the claim that government may not stop a terrorist's speech counseling violence on the Internet, or that members of the Nazi Party may march in some large city. But the "clear and present danger" idea is relatively particular when compared with the claim that nations should adopt the constitutional abstraction "freedom of speech." The term "freedom of speech" is a relative abstraction when measured against the claim that campaign finance laws are acceptable, but the same term is less abstract than the grounds that justify free speech, as in, for example, the principle of personal autonomy or the idea of an unrestricted marketplace of ideas.

In analogical reasoning, this phenomenon occurs all the time. In the law of discrimination, for example, many people think that sex discrimination is "like" race discrimination, and should be treated similarly, even if they lack or cannot agree on a general theory of when discrimination is unacceptable. In the law of free speech, many people agree that a ban on speech by a terrorist or a Communist is "like" a ban on speech by a member of any opposing party, and should be treated similarly – even if they lack or cannot agree on a general theory about the foundations of the free speech principle.

III. Defending Small Steps

A. Incomplete Theorization and Silence

What might be said on behalf of incompletely theorized agreements about the content of a Constitution, or incompletely theorized judgments about particular constitutional cases? What is so good about shallowness? Some people think of incomplete theorization as quite unfortunate – as embarrassing, or reflective of some important problem, or a failure of nerve, or even philistine. When people theorize, by raising the level of abstraction, they do so to reveal bias, or confusion, or inconsistency. Surely participants in politics and constitutional law should not abandon this effort.

There is important truth in these usual thoughts, as we shall see below; it would be senseless to celebrate theoretical modesty at all times and in all contexts. Sometimes participants in constitutional law and politics have sufficient information, and sufficient agreement, to be very ambitious. Sometimes they have to reason ambitiously in order to resolve cases. To the extent that we are able to trust the theoretical capacities of judges, or others, theoretical ambition seems like nothing to lament. But judges are hardly infallible, and incompletely theorized judgments help make constitutions and constitutional law possible. They even help make social life possible. Silence – on something that may prove false, obtuse, or excessively contentious – can help minimize conflict, allow the present to learn from the future, and save a great deal of time and expense. What is said and resolved may be no more important than what is left out. There are a number of points here.

The first and most obvious point is that incompletely theorized agreements about constitutional principles and cases may be necessary for social stability. They are well-suited to a world – and especially a legal world – containing social disagreement on large-scale issues. Stability would be difficult to obtain if fundamental disagreements broke out in every case of public or private dispute. In the nations of Eastern Europe, stable constitution-making has been possible only because the meaning of the document's broad terms has not been specified in advance.

Second, incompletely theorized agreements can promote two goals of a constitutional democracy and a liberal legal system: to enable people to live together, and to permit them to show each other a measure of reciprocity and mutual respect. The use of low-level principles or rules allows judges on multimember bodies and perhaps even citizens generally to find a common way of life without producing unnecessary antagonism. Both rules and low-level principles make it unnecessary to resolve fundamental disagreements. At the same time, incompletely theorized agreements allow people to show each other a high degree of mutual respect, civility, reciprocity, or even charity. Frequently ordinary people disagree in some deep way on an issue – what to do in the Middle East, pornography, same-sex marriages, the war on terror – and sometimes they agree not to discuss that issue much, as a way of deferring to each other's strong convictions and showing a measure of reciprocity and respect (even if they do not at all respect the particular conviction that is at stake). If reciprocity and mutual respect are desirable, it follows that public officials or judges, perhaps even more than ordinary people, should not challenge their fellow citizens' deepest and most defining commitments, at least if those commitments are reasonable and if there is no need for them to do so. Indeed, we can see a kind of political charity in the refusal to contest those commitments when life can proceed without any such contest.

To be sure, some fundamental commitments are appropriately challenged in the legal system or within other multimember bodies. Some such commitments are ruled off-limits by the Constitution itself. Many provisions involving basic rights have this function. Of course it is not always disrespectful to disagree with someone in a fundamental way; on the contrary, such disagreements may sometimes reflect profound respect. When defining commitments are based on demonstrable errors of fact or logic, it is appropriate to contest them. So too when those commitments are rooted in a rejection of the basic dignity of all human beings, or when it is necessary to undertake the contest to resolve a genuine problem. But many cases can be resolved in an incompletely theorized way, and this is the ordinary stuff of constitutional law; that is what I am emphasizing here.

The third point is that for arbiters of social controversies, incompletely theorized agreements have the crucial function of reducing the political cost of enduring disagreements. If participants in constitutional law disavow large-scale theories, then losers in particular cases lose much less. They lose a decision, but not the world. They may win on another occasion. Their own theory has not been rejected or ruled inadmissible. When the authoritative rationale for the result is disconnected from abstract theories of the good or the right, the losers can submit to legal obligations, even if reluctantly, without being forced to renounce their largest ideals.

Fourth, incompletely theorized agreements are especially valuable when a society seeks moral evolution and progress over time. Consider the area of equality, where considerable change has occurred in the past and will inevitably occur in the future. A completely theorized judgment would be unable to accommodate changes in facts or values. If a culture really did attain a theoretical end-state, it would become rigid and calcified; we would know what we thought about everything. Unless the complete theorization were error-free, this would disserve posterity. Hence incompletely theorized agreements are a key to debates over equality in both law and politics, with issues being raised about whether discrimination on the basis of sexual orientation, age, disability, and others are analogous to discrimination on the basis of race; such agreements have the important advantage of allowing a large degree of openness to new facts and perspectives.

At one point, we might think that same-sex relations are akin to incest; at another point, we might find the analogy bizarre. Of course a completely theorized judgment would have many virtues if it is correct. But at any particular moment in time, this is an unlikely prospect for human beings, not excluding judges in constitutional disputes, or those entrusted with the task of creating constitutional provisions.

Compare practical reasoning in ordinary life. At a certain time, you may well refuse to make decisions that seem foundational in character – about, for example, whether to get married within the next year, or whether to have two, three, or four children, or whether to live in London or Paris. Part of the reason for this refusal is knowledge that your understandings of both facts and values may well change. Indeed, your identity may itself change in important and relevant ways, and for this reason a set of firm commitments in advance – something like a fully theorized conception of your life course – would make no sense. Legal systems and nations are not altogether different. I will turn shortly to the limitations of these arguments.

Fifth, shallow rulings seem well-suited to the institutional limits of the federal judiciary, which might well blunder if it tries for theoretical depth. Recall that shallowness can reduce the costs of decisions and the costs of errors. If judges were infallible, and if they had immediate access to the correct theory, there would be little reason to object to depth. But if judges do not think easily or well about theoretical questions, they might avoid depth as a way of minimizing their own burdens while reducing errors.

I am not attempting to defend shallowness in all circumstances. We will soon see that much can be wrong with it. The point is that for a series of reasons, many of them pragmatic, shallowness might be chosen by sensible judges.

B. Burke and His Rationalist Adversaries

Those who emphasize incompletely theorized agreements owe an evident debt to Edmund Burke, who was, in a sense, the great theorist of incomplete theorization. I do not attempt anything like an exegesis of Burke, an exceedingly complex figure, in this space, but let us turn briefly to Burke himself and in particular to his great essay on the French Revolution, in which he rejected the revolutionary temperament because of its theoretical ambition.[4]

Burke's key claim is that the "science of constructing a commonwealth, or reforming it, is, like every other experimental science, not to be taught a priori."[5] To make this argument, Burke opposes theories and abstractions, developed by individual minds, to traditions, built up by many minds over long periods. In his most vivid passage, Burke writes:

> "The science of government being therefore so practical in itself, and intended for such practical purposes, a matter which requires experience, and even more experience than any person can gain in his whole life, however sagacious and observing he may be, it is with infinite caution than any man ought to venture upon pulling down an edifice which has answered in any tolerable degree, for ages the common purposes of society, or on building it up again, without having models and patterns of approved utility before his eyes."[6]

It is for this reason that Burke describes the "spirit of innovation" as "the result of a selfish temper and confined views,"[7] and offers the term "prejudice" as one of enthusiastic approval, noting that "instead of casting away all our old prejudices, we cherish them to a very considerable degree."[8] Emphasizing the critical importance of stability, Burke adds a reference to "the evils of inconstancy and versatility, ten thousand times worse than those of obstinacy and the blindest prejudice."[9] Burke's sharpest distinction, then, is between established practices and individual reason. He contends that reasonable citizens, aware of their own limitations, will effectively delegate decision-making authority to their own traditions. "We are

4 Edmund Burke, Reflections on the Revolution in France, in *The Portable Edmund Burke* (Isaac Kramnick ed.), 1999, 416-451.
5 Id. 442.
6 Id. 451.
7 Id. 428.
8 Id. 451.
9 Id.

afraid to put men to live and trade each on his own private stock of reason," simply "because we suspect that this stock in each man is small, and that the individuals would do better to avail themselves of the general bank and capital of nations, and of ages. Many of our men of speculation, instead of exploding general prejudices, employ their sagacity to discover the latent wisdom which prevails in them."[10]

Burke was enthusiastic about reasoning by analogy, and it is easy to imagine an unambivalently Burkean advocate of incompletely theorized agreements. But Burke's enthusiasm for traditions is contentious, and for good reason. In the aftermath of apartheid, should South Africa have built carefully, and in a tradition-bound way, on its own past? Or should it have adopted a constitution on the basis of some kind of account of human liberty and equality? Social practices, and constitution-making, can be incompletely theorized while also being anti-Burkean. The South African Constitution itself includes stirring and tradition-rejecting ideals of various kinds, and those ideals can be accepted from many different foundations. In constitutional adjudication, judges who believe in incompletely theorized agreements might require government to come up with a reason for its practice – and insist that a tradition, or a longstanding practice, is not itself a reason.

In constitutional law, we can imagine fierce contests between Burkeans and their more rationalist adversaries, even if both camps are willing to march under the banner of incomplete theorization.[11] Those contests cannot be resolved in the abstract; everything depends on the nature of the relevant traditions and the competence of those who propose to subject them to critical scrutiny. If traditions are good, and if the scrutinizers are bad, traditionalism is appealing. If the traditions include injustice and cruelty, and if the scrutinizers are reliable, then traditionalism makes no sense. We shall shortly see how these points bear on theoretical ambition in constitutional law.

C. Narrowness

Now let us turn to narrowness, which is simpler to handle. In some domains of constitutional law, it is certainly best to focus on the particulars and to avoid width. A court might sensibly rule that one exercise of presidential power is unconstitutional, without saying much about other imaginable exercises of presidential power. A court might sensibly rule that sex segregation is impermissible in one domain, without saying much about whether sex segregation might be impermissible in other domains. A court might strike one restriction on speech on the Internet, while also refusing to lay down broad rules governing restrictions of speech

10 Id.

11 For discussion, see Cass R. Sunstein, Burkean Minimalism, 105 *Mich. L. Rev.* (2006) 353.

on the Internet. A court might strike down one restriction on gun ownership under the Second Amendment, while leaving a great deal undecided about the ultimate meaning of that amendment. Recall here Chief Justice Roberts' plea for narrowness and his suggestion that if it is not necessary for a court to say more to decide a case, it is necessary for a court not to say more to decide a case.

But is Chief Justice Roberts correct? Why would sensible judges embrace narrowness? Why, exactly, is it necessary not to say more to decide a case, if it is not necessary to say more to decide a case? We can isolate several reasons. First, institutional reality may require it. On a multimember court, consisting of several (strong-willed?) people, it might be possible to reach a consensus on a particular outcome, but not on a wide rule. Second, wide rulings might impose serious decisional burdens on judges, even if the institutional problem could be overcome. To issue a wide ruling that covers sex segregation, or speech on the Internet, may require judges to ask and answer questions for which they lack relevant information. Third, wide rulings might turn out to embarrass the future. To the extent that courts are in a poor position to generate rules that fit diverse situations, their efforts to do so might produce serious blunders.

These are (yet again) points about the costs of decisions and the costs of errors. But there is an additional point, involving democratic self-government. In the constitutional domain, narrow rules preserve a great deal of space for continuing discussion and debate. Imagine, for example, that a court is asked to issue some wide ruling involving the rights of gays and lesbians or the authority of the President. A refusal to issue that ruling, and a narrow ruling focused on particulars, allows room for continuing argument in the democratic domain. To be sure, a judicial decision that refuses to impose constitutional constraints, and that says (for example) that governments can discriminate against gays and lesbians as they choose, allows democratic space by definition. But in many nations, arguments about morality, and about what government legitimately does, take place in the domain of constitutional argument. In many ways, it is desirable if leaders and citizens generally are permitted to offer their competing views about the meaning of the Constitution itself. For this reason, narrowness can claim democratic justifications.

IV. Against Minimalism

A. Beyond Narrowness

To see what might be wrong with minimalism, let us notice that the points just offered are subject to reasonable objections. In many contexts, they fail to provide an adequate justification of narrowness.

Suppose that a court is operating in a domain where predictability is extremely important – as, for example, because the issue comes up often, because people need guidance, and because it is simply too messy to have to proceed without a sense of what the law is. If this is so, narrow rulings will impose significant decisionmaking burdens on others – and very possibly increase decision costs on balance. Imagine, for example, that the question is the appropriate scope of review of judicial review of agency interpretations of law. That question arises with great frequency, and if a high court does not issue a wide ruling, then lower courts will have to handle a lot of uncertainty. If an area of law is a mess, because of a series of narrow rulings, posterity might be harmed rather than helped.

We can see here a serious problem with Chief Justice Roberts' embrace of unanimous rulings. Roberts favors such rulings in part on the ground that they promote predictability. If the court is not fractured, everyone will know what the law is. But as Roberts also contends, a unanimous ruling is more likely to be narrow, simply because a wide ruling is unlikely to be able to attract a consensus. The problem is that a unanimous, narrow ruling might offer significantly less guidance than a divided, wide ruling. From the standpoint of promoting predictability, it is better, perhaps, to have a 7-2 ruling in favor of some general proposition than a 9-0 ruling in favor of some narrow proposition, limited to particular facts.

It is possible in this light to appreciate certain movements toward width in constitutional law. After decades of grappling with the question of when, exactly, a confession can be said to be voluntary, the Supreme Court issued its wide ruling in the Miranda case – essentially requiring a set of warnings to precede any interrogation.[12] An explanation of this unusually wide step is that the task of deciding on the voluntariness of confessions, on a case-by-case basis, was simply too confusing and difficult. In the interest of clarity and predictability, a wide rule seemed best. Or consider the question whether and when a sexually explicit film should be regulable as "obscenity." After decades of administering a test that invited difficult case-by-case inquiries, the Court adopted for an approach that included greater clarity and width.[13] A defense of that approach is that it greatly reduced decisional burdens, in a way that was justified in light of a) the Court's considerable experience with the problem and b) the frequency with which the issue had arisen.

As a third example, consider the problem of school segregation. For decades, the Court investigated, on a case-by-case basis, the question whether "separate" really was "equal." In ruling that separate was inherently unequal,[14] the Court adopted a general principle about equality, with a degree of theoretical depth to be sure (and I will have something to say about that in a moment). But the Court also issued a wide rule, one that ensured a simple, clear answer to a question that had been pressed repeatedly and been answered only with difficulty.

12 Miranda v. Arizona., 384 US 436 (1966).

13 United States v. Miller, 413 US 15 (1973).

14 Brown v. Bd of Educ. 347 US 483 (1954).

B. Narrowness and Width, Standards and Rules

We should now be able to see that the choice between narrowness and width raises many of the questions raised by the choice between standards and rules, a topic that has produced a large literature.[15] A standard leads a great deal of work to be done by subsequent decision-makers; by contrast, a rule resolves cases in advance, and ensures that the work of subsequent decision-makers is essentially mechanical. For example, a 60 mile per hour speech limit is a rule, whereas a standard might say that a driver must drive in a "reasonable and prudent manner." Under the specified speech limit, it is obvious whether someone has violated the law; under a standard, the judge has to do a fair bit of work to decide that question.

A preference for minimalism is very close, analytically, to a preference for standards over rules. To be sure, the two preferences are not identical. A holding that is governed by a standard is in an important respect narrow, because the standard needs to be specified in particular cases; but a narrow decision need not be a standard at all. Such a decision may even be a rule, restricted to an unusual set of facts; it may not set out a standard of any kind. What I am emphasizing is that by its very nature, a minimalist ruling leaves a great deal undecided, in a way that frees up future decision-makers but also leaves them to some extent at sea. This is exactly the characteristic that distinguishes standards from rules.

A preference for standards makes best sense when it serves to reduce the number and magnitude of errors, and when it serves as well to reduce the aggregate burdens of decision. Suppose again that the Supreme Court is attempting to resolve a difficult question involving, say, the constitutional status of segregation on the basis of sex. The Court might think that it lacks the information that would enable it to set out a sensible rule. It may believe that sex segregation is not acceptable when it excludes women from a valuable educational opportunity, but that it is permissible to have sex-segregated sports teams, and that the legitimacy of sex-segregated high school education presents difficult question. The Court might believe that a simple rule – sex segregation yes, or sex segregation no – would be outrun by reality. It might also believe that a complex rule, specifying the validity of segregation across diverse contexts, is too difficult to specify during an early encounter with the question.[16]

Points of this kind do justify a preference for narrow rulings in many contexts. The problem – the general one for those who favor narrowness – is that there is no reason to think that judges should *systematically* favor standards over rules. Whether standards are desirable, and whether narrowness makes sense, depend on whether the arguments that justify them apply in the particular case. There is no justification for a general presumption in favor of standards or narrowness. The

15 See Louis Kaplow, Rules Versus Standards: An Economic Analysis, 41 *Duke L. J.* (1992), 557.

16 On some of the considerations here, see Cass R. Sunstein, Trimming, *Harv. L. Rev.* (forthcoming 2009).

pragmatic arguments that justify narrowness will often call for its repudiation. I am suggesting, then, that it is often sensible for judges to go beyond minimalism in the form of narrowness, because the pragmatic and democratic arguments that (sometimes) call for small steps often argue strongly in favor of large ones. If judges are concerned with the costs of decisions and the costs of errors, they will often find themselves settling on wide rules.

Let us return to the question of shallowness in this light.

C. Conceptual Ascents: From Shallowness to Depth

Borrowing from Henry Sidgwick's writings on ethical method,[17] a critic of shallowness, in the form of incompletely theorized agreements, might respond that constitutional law should frequently use ambitious theories.[18] For example, there is often good reason for people interested in constitutional rights to raise the level of abstraction and ultimately to resort to large-scale theory. Concrete judgments about particular cases can prove inadequate for morality or constitutional law. Sometimes people do not have clear intuitions about how cases should come out. Sometimes their intuitions are insufficiently reflective. Sometimes seemingly similar cases provoke different reactions, and it is necessary to raise the level of theoretical ambition to explain whether those different reactions are justified, or to show that the seemingly similar cases are different after all. Sometimes people simply disagree.

By looking at broader principles, we may be able to mediate the disagreement. In any case there is a problem of explaining our considered judgments about particular cases, in order to see whether they are not just a product of accident or error. When modest judges join an opinion that is incompletely theorized, they must rely on a reason or a principle, justifying one outcome rather than another. The opinion must itself refer to a reason or principle; it cannot just announce a victor. Perhaps the low-level principle is wrong, because it fails to fit with other cases, or because it is not defensible as a matter of (legally relevant) political morality.

Here is another way to put the point. Sometimes it is burdensome to rule in a theoretically ambitious way, and sometimes shallow decisions can be wrong. A judge who thinks more ambitiously – about, for example, affirmative action, abortion, and discrimination on the basis of sexual orientation – might be able to produce safeguards against blunders. In the abstract, the incompletely theorized agreement may be nothing to celebrate. If a judge is reasoning well, he should have before him a range of other cases, C through Z, in which the principle is tested against others and refined. At least if he is a distinguished judge, he will

17 See Henry Sidgwick, *The Methods of Ethics*. 7th ed., 1966, 96-104.
18 This is the tendency in Ronald Dworkin, *Law's Empire*, 1985.

experience a kind of "conceptual ascent," in which the more or less isolated and small low-level principle is finally made part of a more general theory. Perhaps this would be a paralyzing task, and perhaps our judge need not often attempt it. But it is an appropriate model for understanding law and an appropriate aspiration for evaluating judicial and political outcomes. Judges who insist on staying at a low level of theoretical ambition are philistines, even ostriches.

Return to ordinary life. If someone is unsure what to do with a relationship or a medical problem, he might not do so well if he avoids the foundational questions. If he can answer those questions well, he might be able to choose far more wisely than he will do if he plods along with decisions that are at once narrow and shallow. Something similar seems to be true in the constitutional domain. Indeed, we might go beyond necessity and speak instead of opportunity. Perhaps it is best to see constitutional provisions as positively inviting a degree of depth, and therefore to celebrate those occasions in which courts announce the nature of the foundational commitments that underlie one or another right. In the domain of equality, the ban on racial segregation is not properly taken as a tribute to the importance of predictability. Instead the Court deepened the foundations of the equality norm, essentially seeing it as a ban on government efforts to subordinate an identifiable group. In the domain of sex equality, the Supreme Court has issued a narrow ruling that also offers a degree of depth, because it opts for a particular conception of what the equality principle is about.

At least if they have time and competence, moral and constitutional reasoners thinking about basic rights should be encouraged to attempt a degree of theoretical ambition. In democratic processes, it is appropriate and sometimes indispensable to challenge existing practice in abstract terms. The same is true in constitutional law. And while narrow rulings leave posterity less constrained, the absence of constraint may be a vice, rather than a virtue, if the result is to leave nearly everything up for grabs.

As I have noted, minimalist decisions have many virtues. They might reflect the institutional limits of the judiciary; they can reduce the social costs of disagreement; they seem to demonstrate humility and mutual respect. Both narrowness and shallowness may be critical to successful constitution-making in a pluralistic society. The points bear on constitutional disputes as well. In a well-functioning constitutional democracy, judges are usually reluctant to invoke philosophical abstractions as a basis for invalidating the outcomes of electoral processes. They are reluctant because they know that they may misunderstand the relevant philosophical arguments, and they seek to show respect to the diverse citizens in their nation. A conceptual ascent might be appealing in the abstract, but if those who ascend will blunder, they might stay close to the ground. But as judicial confidence grows, perhaps because of extended experience, the argument for depth grows as well.

I have emphasized theoretical ambition on moral questions, but notice that an interest in depth might push judges to accept a contentious approach that, in particular cases, diminishes their own theory-building obligations. Perhaps judges can be convinced, in one or another domain, that they should not invalidate statutes unless the constitutional violation is clear and unmistakable.[19] This position is certainly controversial, and some of the arguments on its behalf have a degree of theoretical ambition. But if judges accept it, they will not be required to think ambitiously very often. Or consider originalism. Those who argue that judges should be bound by the original meaning often contend that their approach disciplines courts and relieves them from the task of making their own judgments about the nature of liberty or equality.[20] To be sure, we could imagine an incompletely theorized agreement on behalf of originalism, but it seems clear that people will not accept that approach unless they can be persuaded to agree on some foundational questions.

The central point is that methodological disputes are often central to constitutional law. If one or another method is best, and if judges have reason to believe that it is best, they should accept it. Shallowness, on questions of method, may not be possible in the face of dispute, and even if shallowness is possible, it might lead to serious blunders.

D. Fundamentals

Incompletely theorized agreements have many virtues, but the arguments on their behalf cannot be accepted in the abstract. Stability, for example, is brought about by such agreements, and stability is usually desirable; but a constitutional system that is stable and unjust should probably be made less stable. Consider two qualifications to what has been said thus far. Some cases cannot be decided *at all* without introducing a fair amount in the way of theory. Some constitutional cases cannot be decided *well* without introducing more ambitious theory. If a good theory (involving, for example, the right to free speech) is available, and if judges can be persuaded that the theory is good, there should be no taboo on its judicial acceptance.

What of disagreement? The discussion thus far has focused on the value of convergence. In law, as in politics, disagreement can be a productive and creative force, revealing error, showing gaps, moving discussion and results in better directions. Many constitutional orders place a high premium on "government by discussion," and when the process is working well, this is true for the judiciary as well as for other institutions. Existing agreements may be a product of coercion, subtle or not, or of accidents of various kinds, or of a failure of imagination.

Constitutional disagreements have many legitimate sources. Two of these sources are especially important. First, people may share general commitments

19 See Adrian Vermeule, *Judging Under Uncertainty*, 2006.
20 See Antonin Scalia, *A Matter of Interpretation*, 1998.

but disagree on particular outcomes. Second, people's disagreements on general principles may produce disagreement over particular outcomes and low-level propositions as well. People who think that an autonomy principle accounts for freedom of speech may also think that the government cannot regulate truthful, nondeceptive commercial advertising – whereas people who think that freedom of speech is basically a democratic idea, and is focused on political speech, may have no interest in protecting commercial advertising at all. Constitutional theorizing can have a salutary function in part because it tests low-level principles by reference to more ambitious claims. Disagreements can be productive by virtue of this process of testing.

Certainly if everyone having a reasonable general view converges on a particular (by hypothesis reasonable) judgment, nothing is amiss. But if an agreement is incompletely theorized, there is a risk that everyone who participates in the agreement is mistaken, and hence that the outcome is mistaken. There is also a risk that someone who is reasonable has not participated, and that if that person were included, the agreement would break down. Over time, incompletely theorized agreements should be subject to scrutiny and critique, at least in democratic arenas, and sometimes in courtrooms as well. That process may result in more ambitious thinking than constitutional law ordinarily entails.

Social consensus is hardly a consideration that outweighs everything else. Usually it would be much better to have a just outcome, rejected by many people, than an unjust outcome with which all or most agree. A just constitution is more important than an agreed-upon constitution. Consensus or agreement is important largely because of its connection with stability, itself a valuable but far from overriding social goal. It may well be right to make an unjust constitutional order a lot less stable. We have seen that incompletely theorized agreements, even if stable and broadly supported, may conceal or reflect injustice. Certainly agreements should be more fully theorized when the relevant theory is plainly right and people can be shown that it is right, or when the invocation of the theory is necessary to decide cases. None of this is inconsistent with what I have claimed here.

It would be foolish to say that no general theory about constitutional law or rights can obtain agreement, even more foolish to deny that some general theories deserve support, and most foolish of all to say that incompletely theorized agreements warrant respect whatever their content. Shallowness, no less than narrowness, has pragmatic justifications, and in some cases, those justifications will often prove inadequate. It is true that more ambitious decisions create real losers, who will not be pleased to find that their defining commitments have been ruled off-limits. But sometimes the losers deserve to lose. Consider, for example, the width and relative depth reflected in judicial rulings that racial segregation is unconstitutional, that government may not take stands in favor of particular religions, that the president does not have the inherent authority to seize private property, that political speech may not be regulated unless it presents a clear and present danger, that the first amendment sharply restricts use of the common law of libel, and that the equality principle prevents governments from turning the sex difference into a systematic source of social disadvantage.

For good reasons, judgments of this kind are rare. But in the most glorious periods in democratic life, national decisions reflect a high degree of theoretical depth, and they are wide rather than narrow. In crucial moments in American history, the same has been true of constitutional law. Many of those moments deserve celebration, not lament.[21]

21 The qualification is necessary because width and depth can also be found in some of the Court's worst decisions. See, e.g., Lochner v. New York, 198 US 45 (1905); Dred Scott v. Sandford, 60 US 393 (1857).

COMMENTARIES

Yasuo Hasebe, Tokyo, Japan

Incompletely Theorised Rationale for Incompletely Theorised Agreements

Comment on Cass R. Sunstein, Beyond Judicial Minimalism, in: *Judicial Minimalism: For and Against,* Ninth Kobe Lecture, Aoyama Gakuin University, Tokyo, Japan, June 7, 2008.

Cass Sunstein describes the virtues of incompletely theorised agreements, in which the participants are clear on the concrete results of the agreement, but do not agree on the general theory that grounds them. According to Sunstein, such agreements are "well-suited to a world–and especially a legal world–containing social dissensus on large-scale issues."[1]

Such agreements, shallowly founded and narrow in scope, promote social stability by containing social disagreements on large scale issues. They enable people to live together with a measure of mutual respect despite their disagreements, and thus to avoid the cost of enduring conflicts. Such agreements thereby facilitate the progress and moral evolution of a society over time.[2]

However, Sunstein offers an exception to his general argument for such agreements: there must be one large-scale theory that prescribes that participants in law favour incompletely theorised agreements.[3]

I agree that incompletely theorised agreements have many virtues in law, particularly in a pluralistic society with a relatively well-functioning, stable constitution. However, I do see a need to clarify the character of his general claim, in regard to which I would like to raise two points.

First, the argument that Sunstein offers for incompletely theorised agreements in law is itself not completely theorised. It is composed of various rationales which do not sit together easily, and the scope of application of these rationales is not neatly demarcated. Second, there seems to be no reason why we need a completely theorised rationale for incompletely theorised agreements in law.

Within the argument that Sunstein offers for incompletely theorised agreements, at least three different rationales are discernable: (1) a utilitarian rationale for sticking with social practices or rules that actually solve co-ordination problems in a given society; (2) a Wittgensteinian rationale for respecting the traditional practices with which we make sense of social life; and (3) a prudential ra-

1 Cass R. Sunstein, *Legal Reasoning and Political Conflicts,* 1996, 39.

2 Cass R. Sunstein, Beyond Judicial Minimalism, in: *Judicial Minimalism: For and Against,* Ninth Kobe Lecture, 2008, 12-13.

3 Sunstein (note 1), 60-61.
In Sunstein (note 2), 1, Sunstein rightly stresses that the validity of this general claim for preferring incompletely theorised agreements has its limits.

tionale for not aspiring too highly in a multi-valued, changing society in which time and capacity are limited.[4] Note that Sunstein himself does not distinguish between these rationales; these are my distinctions. Among the three rationales, Sunstein refers explicitly neither to (1) nor (2), but both are congruent with his analysis.

The first of these rationales, the utilitarian, is well-known.[5] There are many occasions when most people want to behave as most other people behave, but no one is sure how other people behave. If such a situation happens recurrently, a convention emerges that indicates how people are to behave. Quite often, there is no reasonable ground for the particular course of conduct conventionally indicated, but if most people take that course, it is rational for everyone to do so as well. In such cases, only incompletely theorised agreements are possible, since there is no theoretical reason for people to take the indicated course. Nevertheless, it is reasonable for all participants to do so.[6] Such agreements enable the stability of social life for millions of people, who cannot communicate with one another one-by-one to solve their co-ordination problems.[7]

However, this utilitarian rationale does not sit easily with Sunstein's reference to the "wisdom of crowds," and in particular, to the Condorcet Jury Theorem,[8] since these arguments presuppose that the relevant questions have objective, "right answers." If our task is to find a salient practice which solves a co-ordination problem, there is no need for recourse to a majority-decision, or for pooling a large amount of knowledge of the multitudes. Any course of conduct that can become a focus of people's expectations will do.

In discussing the "wisdom of crowds," and in stressing the importance of "fixed points" in law, Sunstein may be thinking of the second rationale, the Wittgensteinian justification of social practices.[9] The body of conventions shared by a community of lawyers, and used as "fixed points" in their arguments, consists

4 Sunstein regards the fact that the judiciary is composed of multiple members as a reason for it to favour incompletely theorised agreements (Sunstein (note 2), 8; Sunstein (note 1), 39 and 192). But the legislature, the typical organ of the political branch, comprises many more members with varied political views than the judiciary. Reasons for the judiciary to prefer incompletely theorised agreements might better be sought in its limited capacity than in its multiple-member composition.

5 I draw here on Edna Ullmann-Margalit, *The Emergence of Norms*, 1977, Ch. III; John Finnis, *Natural Law and Natural Rights*, 1980, Ch. IX; Gerald Postema, Co-ordination and Convention at the Foundations of Law, *Journal of Legal Studies*, Vol. 11 (1982), 165-203.

6 Rules issued by public authorities, which also become focal points of incompletely theorized agreements, may solve co-ordination problems as well.

7 Jeremy Waldron points out that much of Edmund Burke's critique against human rights can be understood in utilitarian terms, especially when Burke recommends following traditional custom on the ground that it "makes it easier for people to co-ordinate and plan their activity" (Jeremy Waldron, ed., *Nonsense upon Stilts: Bentham, Burke and Marx on the Rights of Man*, 1987, 84-90).

8 Sunstein (note 2), 7, note 7; cf. Cass Sunstein, *Infotopia,* 2006, 25 ff.

9 I elaborate on this conception in Yasuo Hasebe, The Rule of Law and Its Predicament, *Ratio Juris*, Vol. 17, No. 4, 2004, 489-500.

not only of general principles but also of answers to particular questions that most lawyers in the community intuitively regard to be correct.[10] It would be exceedingly difficult to construct a coherent system of general legal principles that accords with and justifies these concrete answers, or even a part of them, particularly in a pluralistic contemporary society in which diverse, incommensurable values compete with one another. In such a context, a full perspective that encompasses the labyrinthine legal landscape is unattainable. It is possible, however, to find *intermediate cases* that connect different "fixed points" by using analogical reasoning, rather than to summon an all-embracing, coherent philosophical theory.[11]

In this conception, each concrete answer to a legal question indicates a right answer without providing deep or wide justification. This conception therefore seems to accord with Sunstein's reference to the "wisdom of crowds." It is also congruent with some elements of Burkean advocacy for obedience to the traditional "prejudices" of society, rather than for individual calculation in rational terms[12].

The third, prudential rationale for incompletely theorised agreements is also detectable in Sunstein's argument. This rationale focuses on our limited time and resources for finding enduring answers to moral questions in a changing environment. By restricting the scope and foundation of our agreements, we can better adapt to circumstances and progress in our moral evolution.[13] Following precedent liberates us from the need for wide-ranging and far-reaching theoretical bases for our agreements.

This rationale is different from the first two. If our capacity is as limited as must be assumed under this rationale, then we cannot easily conclude that we face a co-ordination problem, nor would we be able to find a right answer by a majority-decision or more generally have recourse to the "wisdom of the multitudes."

In short, what Sunstein offers is not a complete theory for incompletely theorised agreements. It is a combination of different, not entirely compatible rationales for incompletely theorised agreements. We need not lament this, however; there is no need for a complete theory of incompletely theorised agreements. We

10 Sunstein points out that in analogical reasoning in law, "source cases" operate as entirely "fixed points" and are not easily revisable (Sunstein (note 2), 9; Sunstein (note 1), 42 and 92).

11 Cf. Ludwig Wittgenstein, *Philosophical Investigations*, 2001, s. 122.

12 As to Sunstein's analysis of analogical reasoning (Sunstein (note 2), 8-9; Sunstein (note 1), 62-69), it should be added that principles bridging "source" cases and "target" cases are not always to be articulated explicitly. As Gerald Postema points out, if every exercise of judgment of similarity requires an explicit guiding principle, then, no judgment or reasoning is possible. If every such judgment presupposes an explicit principle to guide it, we would be caught in an infinite regress, which Lewis Carroll describes in his dialogue between Achilles and Tortoise (Gerald Postema, Analogical Thinking in Law, in: *Common Law Theory*, ed. Douglas Edlin, 2007, 114; cf. Robert Brandom, *Making It Explicit*, 1994, 20-23). While different people may presuppose different bridging principles, we may still achieve an agreed solution to the "target" case.

13 Sunstein (note 2), 13; Sunstein (note 1), 42 and 99.

can, and we should, be satisfied with an incompletely theorised agreement for incompletely theorised agreements.

Yasuo Hasebe
School of Law
University of Tokyo
Tokyo, Japan

Makoto Usami, Tokyo, Japan*

Shallow Grounds for Shallow Judicial Decision: A Response to Sunstein

Comment on Cass R. Sunstein, "Beyond Judicial Minimalism," in Judicial Minimalism: For and Against, Ninth Kobe Lecture, Aoyama Gakuin University, Tokyo, June 7, 2008.

In his paper presented at the Kobe Lecture and his numerous publications, Cass Sunstein describes and defends a remarkable current tendency found in the Supreme Court of the United States: judicial minimalism.[1] His discussion of this phenomenon is both descriptive and normative. His depiction of some judicial decisions as minimalist seems plausible, although the extent to which this depiction is pertinent as the general picture of a significant portion of judicial practices in the Court is an empirical question that I do not intend to explore here. My main interest lies in the normative aspect of his argument. My comments on Sunstein's discussion are also focused in another way. He makes a distinction between the narrowness dimension and the shallowness dimension of minimalism. In this response, I will mainly discuss shallowness and only briefly mention narrowness.

How can shallow judicial decisions be justified? The arguments Sunstein offers in favor of shallow judgments seem to fall into two categories: prudential and principled. Obviously, individual judges have a prudential reason for shallowness: it would reduce the opportunity cost of their decision making to refrain from elaborating and expressing their deep, abstract, and often far-reaching theories. It is less evident, however, that the judiciary as a whole has good reason for the general rule of shallowness. In the context of narrowness, Sunstein notes that a minimalist judgment might increase the total decision cost by imposing decision-making burdens on others[2]. That is also the case regarding shallowness. A shallow decision made by one judge might thrust the difficult task of deciding deep questions upon other judges in future cases; consequently, the shallowness rule might raise the total decision cost in the long term.

* My thanks are due to Takashi Kanazawa for his detailed suggestions on an earlier version of the present comment. I also benefited from discussions with Yasuo Hasebe, Tatsuo Inoue, and Itaru Shimazu. The usual disclaimer applies.

1 Cass R. Sunstein, "Beyond Judicial Minimalism," in Judicial Minimalism: For and Against, Ninth Kobe Lecture, Aoyama Gakuin University, Tokyo, June 7, 2008. His works on judicial minimalism include *One Case at a Time: Judicial Minimalism on the Supreme Court* (Cambridge, Mass.: Harvard University Press, 1999); *Radicals in Robes: Why Extreme Right-Wing Courts Are Wrong for America* (New York: Basic Books, 2005). For an idea closely related to judicial minimalism–incompletely theorized agreements–see Cass R. Sunstein, *Legal Reasoning and Political Conflict* (New York: Oxford University Press, 1996).

2 Sunstein, "Beyond Judicial Minimalism," 16.

More controversial are the principled reasons for shallow decisions that Sunstein provides, only three of which I shall examine. The first concerns the fallibility of judges. Here we need to distinguish between the possibility of making a mistake in developing a deep and abstract theory and the probability of doing so. When he says that "judges are hardly infallible,"[3] Sunstein appears to mean the possibility rather than the probability. If he intended to argue that the possibility of false reasoning by judges provides a ground for shallowness, then such an argument would be implausible, because judges, who are no less fallible than other decision makers, might err at the shallow level as well as the deep one. Therefore, his argument based on fallibility should be interpreted to mean that in many areas of law the probability of judicial mistake is, at the fundamental level, high enough to recommend shallow decisions. The problem is then that in some cases, one cannot presumably answer the question of whether a judge made a mistake of reasoning in a particular case, unless the judge discloses the full reasoning by which she drew her conclusion. In easy cases–when the void-for-vagueness doctrine is evidently available, for example–a shallow ground may suffice for the assessment of the judge's reasoning by other judges, lawyers, and citizens; however, in hard cases a deep theory may be necessary.

The second argument offered by Sunstein refers to the fact that analogical thinking is pervasive in legal reasoning. After noting this fact, he insists that those engaged in analogical reasoning try to avoid foundational theories.[4] However, the fact of common employment of analogy in law is more than consistent with the significance of deep judicial decision. Analogy occasionally requires deepness. Suppose that a judge faces a case C^*, which involves five characteristics (s, t, u, v, w), and that she finds two apparently relevant past cases C_1 and C_2. C_1 also has five characteristics (s, t, u, v, x), and C_2 has three (w, y, z). Does analogical reasoning require her to recognize the decision in C_1 as a legitimate precedent? Not necessarily. If the weight of w is so overwhelming that the resemblance between C_2 and C^* in terms of w, both individually and totally, overweighs the likeness between C_1 and C^* in s, t, u, and v, then the right precedent of C^* is the decision in C_2, not in C_1. The question then arises how this judge can show, to establish her decision, that w is much more significant than s, t, u, and v. By employing her own deep theory. Only by developing and presenting her profound convictions on the purposes and functions of law in the area in question, can she explain the degree of significance that each of s, t, u, v, and w has in C^*. Of course, she might be mistaken, but unless she relinquishes analogical thinking, she must take the risk of making a mistake.

The third principled argument invokes the idea of democracy.[5] Shallow judicial decisions, Sunstein suggests, tend to trigger or improve the process of demo-

3 Ibid., 11.
4 Ibid., 8-9.
5 The argument grounded on democracy is clearly stated in Sunstein, *One Case at a Time*, 24-45, 259-263.

cratic deliberation, not merely by leaving controversial political issues open but by promoting the legislative debate. True, the judicial techniques he recommends, which are all shallow–for instance, the void-for-vagueness doctrine, the nondelegation doctrine, and the desuetude doctrine–can facilitate the legislative discussion. To establish that shallow judicial decisions in general encourage democratic deliberation, however, he must claim that deep decisions generally discourage it. Such a claim would be readily comprehensible if it was grounded on what I call the hierarchical model of democracy. On this model, the Supreme Court has the final voice in a legal system: once the Court invalidates some statute, the legislature is not permitted to overrule that decision by enacting a new law that could circumvent the alleged deficit of the original statute. However, the hierarchical model does not explain institutional arrangements or political realities in the United States. A more accurate picture of American democracy might be the horizontal model. This model maintains that if the Supreme Court strikes down a statute, the legislature chooses between two courses of reaction: legislators may challenge that decision by making a more sophisticated statute, or they may submit themselves to it. To challenge the Supreme Court's decision is obviously costly, but in a democracy, legislators representing citizens could carry their goals through if they tackled their challenges straight on. On the horizontal model of democracy, we might say, the legislature and the judiciary are involved in a continuous dialogue over public issues through their enactments and judgments. If the Court provides an ambitious justification for its decision, the justification will promote rather than prevent the legislature-judiciary dialogue.

Sunstein cautiously appends supplements and concessions to his central argument, but it is doubtful that they successfully refine the argument. First, he takes the case of the United States Sentencing Commission as an example of shallow agreements reached by judges.[6] The members of the Commission, who were sharply divided on the goals of criminal sentencing, abandoned deep theories and adopted a shallow rule, by agreeing to base any Guidelines on actual past practice. However, the analogy does not work between the case of ex ante rule making and that of ex post decision making. In the former case, no events to which a possible rule will be applied have yet happened, and neither winners nor losers are identified through the process of rule making. Therefore, it may be reasonable to lay down rules without any foundational rationales, when the rule makers excessively diverge on the rationales. In the latter case, the event in question has already happened, and a decision defines who is a winner and who is a loser in the dispute. Decision makers are morally obliged to give reasons for their decision to the loser; not infrequently, it is expected that the reasons will be deep. It is also noteworthy that the situation of the Commission's members – the circumstance in which the rule makers disagree on abstract principles and high theories – seems more or less similar to that of legislators. Members of Congress belong to one or the other of

6 Sunstein, "Beyond Judicial Minimalism," 6-7.

the two opposing parties; they are elected in different states and districts therein; they are supported by diverse social groups and political organizations. It might well stem from these differences that lawmakers sharply diverge on a number of moral and political issues. Given the diversity of views and values among legislators, it is far from clear why judges should, in principle, leave these issues in the hands of lawmakers through their frequent shallow decisions.

Second, Sunstein carefully adds several provisos to his general recommendation of shallow judicial decision. The most remarkable proviso reads, "[i]f a good theory … is available, and if judges can be persuaded that the theory is good, there should be no taboo on its judicial acceptance."[7] The question is this: how can judges be convinced that one particular theory is good, if they did not previously display their own basic convictions and deliberate over fundamental issues? He suggests that if judges in a multimember court happen to discover one good theory, then they should step over the line of shallowness and invoke the theory in deciding the case at hand. To recognize one theory among others as the good one, however, the judges must have got involved in debating deep issues in advance.

In sum, Sunstein correctly describes the tendency of judicial minimalism, including its shallowness aspect, and he cogently provides some prudential reasons for it. The principled reasons he offers in behalf of shallowness are, however, less convincing than they appear at first glance. Moreover, his supplementary and concessive arguments go beyond his own intent and come to illustrate some reasons against the general rule of shallow decisions. Perhaps he is right in arguing that a considerable portion of judicial practices in the Supreme Court is explained in terms of shallowness, but such a situation might be lamentable rather than praiseworthy. In a pluralistic society, judges who hold conflicting views on foundational issues are frequently–more frequently than Sunstein concedes–required to leave the safe trench of shallow technicalities and turn to the battlefield of deep theories.

Makoto Usami
Department of Social Engineering
Graduate School of Decision Science and Technology
Tokyo Institute of Technology
Tokyo, Japan

7 Ibid., 19.

Takehiro Ohya, Nagoya, Japan

Is There Any Need for the Judges to Go Further?

Comment on Cass R. Sunstein, Beyond Judicial Minimalism, in: *Judicial Minimalism: For and Against,* Ninth Kobe Lecture, Aoyama Gakuin University, Tokyo, Japan, June 7, 2008.

1. On Where People Disagree?

Consider a person with inverse spectrum vision; his eyes capture the green light when we see the red light, or he could be impressed by the deep orange sea surrounding tropical islands. The question is whether we agree or disagree in seeing the color of certain objects. Although his eyes noticed the green light rays, he surely will stop at the red light, because he has been trained to stop at seeing what we call "the red signal," which he recognizes from birth as what we call "green" light. We could agree how beautiful today's flaming "orange" sunshine is; while our eyes capture the orange solar rays and his, sky blue. From God's viewpoint, we may be in total discordance in our vision. But, how can we, mere human beings, recognize the utter difference laid in the foundation of our communication? How can we probe that our neighbor captures the same spectrum as we do, or even probe our own accordance?

Professor Sunstein noticed that in many cases "people can agree that a certain practice is or is not constitutional, even when the theories that underlie their judgments sharply diverge." My question here is whether we can confirm such differences as existing. This point can develop twofold: the abstract concept and the specific conceptions.

Let us take the example of comparing equality and liberty, which Professor Sunstein mentions as our disagreement over abstract issues. Is there anyone who refutes the importance of equality when asked in a very abstract manner? According to Professor Amartya Sen, every political conception admits the importance of equality, because it must contain the request for the equal distribution by certain standards.[1] Even libertarianism can be interpreted as the request for equal distribution of controlling power over goods, which every citizen once held.[2] The situation will be almost the same in relation to liberty. In their most abstract sense, almost everyone can agree on the importance of these values. Of course, the problem is that all of these values cannot go together in specific situations,

1 *See*, Amartya Kumar Sen, *Inequality Reexamined,* 1992.

2 Some extreme political conceptions could be exceptions to Professor Sen's analysis. One example is egoism, in the sense Professor Tatsuo Inoue described. *See*, Tatsuo Inoue, *Kyōsei no* s*ahō: kaiwa to shite no* s*eigi* [Manners for Conviviality: Justice as Conversation], 1986, ch. 2 (in Japanese).

since the world we live in does not exist under a manna economy. If our disagreement comes from such incompatibility, from the scarcity of resources, in most cases judicial minimalism would be justified, since its expected role is to make coordination between shared values in certain specific situations.[3] And there will not be so much social demand for judges to go further.

2. How Restrictive The Rules Are?

The argument above, however, can sound like an escape from the point. One could say, for instance, the agreement in an abstract respect of values does not guarantee anything, since such values must be interpreted or applied to specific situations, and, we strongly disagree on how we should interpret them in each case. But, this will cause a more troublesome problem. If we admit the possibility that our interpretations over values may differ, and there is no easy way to determine which interpretation is right, then so it will be with our interpretation over rules or standards. To determine what the previous case means in the current situation, we need to interpret it. Since our disagreement is in the interpretation process, the previous case cannot concretely decide which opinion is the right answer. As a result, our agreement whether "a certain practice is or is not constitutional" cannot guarantee anything on the next conflict.[4]

In this light, there is no difference between rules and standards; any rule needs to be interpreted in its application, just as any standard. Once we admit the possibility that we differ in interpretation, we cannot hide from its danger, unless it stays unwritten.[5] Everything needs to be interpreted, so the meaning of every written text cannot be determinate in itself. Without help of, say, interpretive com-

3 Of course we can imagine the society in which some harshly separated groups with incompatible fundamental values exist. In such cases, however, the main problem will be whether they can organize one unified government. In other words, the question is not what the constitution means, but whether to join in constitutional relations. *See*, Takehiro Ohya, *Kenpō towa seiji o wasureru tame no ruuru de aru: rinen kara, kimekata no ronri e* [Constitution as the Rule to Forget about Politics: from Idea to Logic of Determination], *Ratio*, no. 4, 2007 (in Japanese).

4 The most famous description of this Rule-Following Problem could be that of Ludwig Wittgenstein. *See*, Ludwig Wittgenstein, *Philosophische Untersuchungen*, 1953, esp. §185. Relying mainly on the interpretation of *Philosophiche Untersuchungen* §201, Professor Saul Kripke indicated his sceptical paradox, which influenced many thinkers in Critical Legal Studies with regard to legal interpretation. *See*, Saul A. Kripke, *Wittgenstein on Rules and Private Language: An Elementary Exposition,* 1982. *See* also, eg. Dennis M. Patterson (ed.), *Wittgenstein and Legal Theory,* 1992. On critical investigation over Professor Kripke's "sceptical solution" and its criticism, *see* Takehiro Ohya, *Hōkaishaku no gengo tetsugaku: kuripuki kara kongenteki kiyakushugi e* [On Justifiability of Legal Interpretation: from S. Kripke to Radical Conventionalism], 2006, esp. ch. 3 (in Japanese).

5 That is why Professor Kripke finally relied on some kind of intuition, or "surveyable (übersichtlich)" proof that works without being written. The same tactics to avoid foundational rules being written can be seen in Professor Stanley Fish's argument against the criticism from Professor Owen M. Fiss. *See*, Owen M. Fiss, Objectivity and Interpretation, 34 *Stanf. L. Rev.* 4

munities, justification condition, or something else, we cannot decide how far the specific text determines our next step of application.

The two axes Professor Sunstein indicated, on the depth and width of adjudication, require that the meaning of each text be somewhat determinate. But, if we admit this premise, at least in democratic developed countries, it would be better to consider that we are in broad agreement on fundamental values, which leads judges to minimalism. Once we doubt such determinacy, we cannot help falling to utter indeterminacy. In both ways, the foundation of two axes disappears, in my view.

3. What Is The Function Of Adjudication?

For the latter choice, there must be a question on the function or importance of adjudication: if one interpretation or adjudication cannot restrict or decide our next interpretation, why should we build the judicial system and think that certain interpretations are "authoritative" and we cannot ignore them? My answer is, adjudications are message.

Each application of rules is in itself creating a new convention, and there is nothing but our belief that supports such creation. This position is called "radical conventionalism."[6] We believe that 2 plus 2 is 4, and just because we believe so, 2 plus 2 is 4. When a student doubts that and insists 2 plus 2 is 5, we are in danger of separation. And the word "we" here means a group of beings that share certain beliefs and actions based on those beliefs. In typical civil conflict, the fact that two parties do not share the same interpretation of a certain contract, and thus act in accordance, is its cause.

We must notice two additional beliefs; that our system of beliefs has integrity, and that some judgments are "authoritative." By describing certain interpretations as a part of the system of beliefs we share from before, each adjudication tries to unify our belief, and thus unite us. Although the judges build the next step, they describe it as a part of, or a natural continuation of, preexisting systems of belief. And, believing that the understanding suggested in adjudication is to be shared among society will help our system of beliefs become integral. So, the value of adjudication depends on whether it succeeds to reunite "us".

Please note that it does not mean that the next step (the adjudication) is restricted or decided from the preexisting chain of adjudications; the new interpretation is always free. Or, describing from the viewpoint of a judge, he is just under

(1982). *See* also, Stanley Fish, Fish v. Fiss, 36 *Stanf. L. Rev.* 6 (1984). On the similarity of these tactics, *see* Ohya (note 7), esp. 97-99, calling it "invisible foundationalism."

6 In investigating the Rule-Following Problem, Professor Shigeki Noya proposed this position. *See*, Shigeki Noya, *Kongenteki kiyakushugi: ronshō no ikiru ba to shite no ronri* [Radical Conventionalism: Logic as the stage for proof], *Gendai Shisō,* 1990, Oct., (in Japanese). On its relevance to legal philosophy, *see* Ohya (note 7), esp. ch. 4.

pressure from the expectation that he should gain the agreement of the general public *after* he issued certain adjudications. So, he could issue very inventive adjudications if he expects very positive recognition from the public, or even more aggressive ones if he wishes to be recognized by future historians, or whomever. Adjudications are the proposals, or even temptations, for us to keep unified.

The common consensus among lawyers that most adjudication needs to be minimal is based on the history we share; we were born and brought up in strong, well-established systems of beliefs. Lawyers, in addition, are trained to embody a special system of beliefs, which is usually called the legal mind. Again, I would like to say that our disagreement comes from our fundamental, deep agreement.

There are chances, however, that we notice deep splits or differences in our system of beliefs. The attitude over segregation could be one clear example. And it is true that in that case the famous adjudication of the United States Supreme Court reunites the whole society, at least with some twenty or thirty years of struggle. But these great adjudications, with deep reasoning and broad judging, are required to mend larger and fundamental conflict within society. The reunification there had political meaning, just like building a new constitution. The adjudications went beyond minimalism, not just mending our small rip in systems of beliefs but establishing a new set, belonging to the political sphere, rather than the judicial.

4. How Far Can Judges Go?

These points lead us to the question; how far can judges, or the judicial branch as a whole, go beyond minimalism? From the viewpoint that sees adjudication as a message, the most important factor to answer the question is their political legitimacy. At least, Professor Sunstein will also admit that on "great" situations in which the justices issued wide judgment with deep reasoning and sent clear messages to reunite the general public which suffered severe conflict over a certain issue, such adjudications contain huge political meaning. Such great cases like *Brown v. Board of Education*, or *Roe v. Wade*, changed the fundamental structure of American society, and thus can be thought to have huge constitutional value. Such adjudications demonstrate the political power of judges to change society. But, does such power not originally belong to the legislative branch, or the statesmen who consist the Houses of legislature? Why can judges make use of such power? Where did they receive their legitimacy to send such "great" messages to society? Here we come to the question over the political legitimacy of judges, and we can see very large differences on this point.

In the United States, judges are expected to keep their *political neutrality*, and it means at the same time that they are political. Of course, I do not intend to say that they are politically biased or unfairly controlled, but as the nomination of the justice of the Supreme Court usually starts severe political debate within and outside of the Senate, the personal affairs of the judicial branch cannot be independent from politics. In some states, judges are selected by direct election, sometimes under the clear declaration of the candidates' political position. In short, they are expected to have neutrality under political control, but no one doubts that they have their own political stance.

The American judges are political; so it will be OK for their messages to have political meanings. Their power is granted by direct (in some states) or indirect (in federal courts, *etc.*) political process and political discussions or deliberations.

On the other hand, when Japanese judges are expected to be independent from politics, it means mainly that they should be separate from any political stance, whether it is currently in their governing position or not. In one famous case, an associate judge was disciplined by the Supreme Court for his attendance at a symposium in which the organizers openly declared their opposition for a cabinet bill.[7] At first, the associate judge was invited to the symposium as a panelist, but since he was cautioned by the Court to not endanger his neutrality, he abandoned the invitation and instead joined as an ordinary attendant. The Court, however, decided that his remark about the course of affairs from the floor had its connotation against the bill and endangered the "fair and neutral judiciary."

In other words, Japanese judges are expected to keep their *apolitical neutrality*. Although the cabinet holds the power to nominate the judges, its process usually happens in a very bureaucratic way. The justices of the Supreme Court are counted, for instance, not by their political position but their original career; six from lower court judges, four from practicing attorneys, two from public prosecutors, and so on. The nomination of new justices hugely depends on the will of the group to which the retired justice belonged. When a justice from practicing attorneys retires, the candidate is usually sent from the bar associations. They are expected to have a professional background, not political. The legitimacy of Japanese judges comes not from the direct political procedure, but from the system to which they belong.

My question here is, under such apolitical neutrality, and at the same time without political legitimacy under direct or indirect democratic deliberation, is there any chance for Japanese judges to go beyond minimalism? Should they not keep their silence over political matters and thus abandon sending "great" messages? Is it not their duty to leave things open to the debates and discussions in the Houses of legislature by relying upon judicial minimalism? Of course, I do not intend to deny the importance of Professor Sunstein's theory on the American judicial model, but if the answers are "yes," its scope will be limited – at least in the countries with career judges, the applicability is doubtful. I am now won-

7 Decision of the Supreme Court Grand Bench, 1st of Dec., 1997 (*Minji Saiban Reishū* [Civil Case Precedents], vol. 52, no. 9, pp. 1761). The original decision of the High Court, which had the jurisdiction over the disciplinary proceeding against the concerned associate judge, was approved by 10 to 5.

dering about its value and possibility in foreign (from an American viewpoint) legal systems.

Takehiro Ohya
Graduate School of Law
Nagoya University
Nagoya, Japan

Hirohide Takikawa,* Tokyo, Japan

Beyond Judicial Minimalism, And Then Where to Go?

Comment on Cass R. Sunstein, Beyond Judicial Minimalism, in: *Judicial Minimalism: For and Against,* Ninth Kobe Lecture, Aoyama Gakuin University, Tokyo, Japan, June 7, 2008.

1. Incompletely Theorized Agreements

Cass R. Sunstein's legal theory starts from the significance of incompletely theorized agreements. Sunstein maintains that "incompletely theorized agreements play a pervasive role in law and society."[1] Hence our first task is to analyze incompletely theorized agreements.

A. Incompleteness, Theorization, and Agreements

Incompletely theorized agreements consist of three elements: incompleteness, theorization, and agreements. First, incompletely theorized agreements are *incompletely* theorized agreements, that is, full theorization is unnecessary, or sometimes undesirable, for society. Complete theorization is often beyond human capacities and a source of controversy. The emphasis on incompletely theorized agreements involves anti-theory or anti-principle positions. Second, incompletely theorized agreements are agreements that are to some extent *theorized.* Incompletely theorized agreements are different from non-theorized agreements. When we have diverse opinions on an issue, voting will create a kind of agreement; voting by nine judges in the Supreme Court of the United States will inevitably form a majority opinion consisting of five or more judges. However, simple congruence in the final conclusion is not seen as an incompletely theorized agreement because it is not based on any supporting rationale. While Sunstein refers to "full particularity," that is, an agreement on a result without agreeing on any justification, he avoids focusing on the limiting case.[2] The insistence on incompletely theorized agreements relates to anti-voting or perhaps anti-majority rule positions. Third,

* Research for this paper was supported by Grants-in-Aid for Scientific Research (C) 20530010 from Japan Society for the Promotion of Science.

1 Cass R. Sunstein, *Legal Reasoning and Political Conflict*, 1996, 35.

2 Cass R. Sunstein, Beyond Judicial Minimalism, in: *Judicial Minimalism: For and Against*, Ninth Kobe Lecture, 2008, 4. Sunstein seems to characterize full particularity as a kind of incompletely theorized agreement. Full particularity, however, is better seen as a completely non-theorized agreement because it is much harder to justify than an incompletely theorized agreement.

incompletely theorized agreements are *agreements*, which are reached over social disagreements. Incompletely theorized agreements are better than disagreements because they can assuage social conflicts. Agreements play a decisive role in keeping social stability and establishing political legitimacy.

Incompletely theorized agreements are of two kinds: agreements on abstractions and agreements on particular outcomes.[3] While agreements on general principles play a major role in constitution-making, agreements on concrete results acquire much more interest of legal theorists.

B. Two Grounds for Incompletely Theorized Agreements

Full theorization is usually regarded as superior to incomplete theorization. It is thus important to examine why incompletely theorized agreements have significant social uses. Sunstein offers several reasons that explain the value of incompletely theorized agreements: they may be necessary for social stability, especially in a world containing social disagreements; they enable people to live together and to show mutual respect; they reduce the political cost of disagreements; they help moral evolution over time; and they are necessary because of people's limited time and capacities.[4]

These considerations can be classified into two groups: reasonable pluralism and bounded capacity. The first factor, reasonable pluralism, is basically based on the problems of political liberalism. The main question for John Rawls in his *Political Liberalism* is to find the conditions under which we can live together given the fact of reasonable pluralism. [5] It is fundamental to examine the means to reach social stability or "social peace"[6] in a world where the conceptions of a good life are pluralistically diverse. In the face of diverse comprehensive views, the idea of an overlapping consensus plays an important role in achieving stability and social agreement. Although Sunstein claims that the notion of incompletely theorized agreements and the idea of an overlapping consensus are "far from the same,"[7] there exists no doubt a similarity between them: both attempt to reduce the intensity of social conflicts. Furthermore, they enable people to show mutual respect toward each other in the sense that people's deepest commitments should not be challenged.

The second factor, limited capacity, has several aspects. First, people are restrained by time. People have less time than they need for complete theorization.

3 In Sunstein (note 1), ch.2, Sunstein distinguishes three kinds of incompletely theorized agreements: an agreement on a general principle, an agreement on a mid-level principle, and an agreement on a particular outcome. The distinction between the former two is less important than the distinction between the two and the last one.

4 Sunstein (note 2), 11; Sunstein (note 1), 41

5 John Rawls, *Political Liberalism*, 1995.

6 Cass R. Sunstein, Burkean Minimalism, 105 *Mich. L. Rev.* 353 (2006), 365.

7 Sunstein (note 1), 47.

Second, people often have trouble with abstractions. People are familiar with concrete and particular facts surrounding them; they are less familiar with abstract and universal principles.

Sunstein emphasizes incompletely theorized agreements partly because they "fit" our social practices. Incompletely theorized agreements have a descriptive value because they are a general phenomenon. As Sunstein states, "incompletely theorized agreements play a pervasive role in constitutional law and in democracy generally." [8] What we call "iridescent agreements," or equivocal concurrence, are often utilized in politics to reach a temporal conclusion. We can observe them not only in courts but also in politics and even in ordinary life.

Here comes the question: How does judicial minimalism follow from the significance of incompletely theorized agreements? What exactly is the relationship between judicial minimalism and incomplete theorization? Does the latter justify the former?

2. Judicial Minimalism

Judicial minimalism is the claim that judges do and should prefer small steps to larger ones when they interpret the constitution. Minimalists emphasize the need for judges to pay careful attention to the particulars of individual cases and the established tradition. Minimalist judges seek rulings that are shallow rather than deep. They tend to decide a case without resolving the fundamental issues, or without completely theorizing the particular conclusions. Shallowness is the common feature of various kinds of minimalism.[9]

Sunstein presents minimalism as a theory of judicial review, not as a theory of the Constitution or a theory of law in general. He maintains that minimalism is far better than other approaches such as majoritarianism, originalism, and perfectionism.[10] The reasons why judicial minimalism is superior to other approaches are closely connected with the grounds why incompletely theorized agreements are practically significant. Both reasonable pluralism and limited capacity are relevant here.

A. Stability

Judicial minimalism can achieve social stability in a world where social disagreements exist on large-scale issues. As we discussed the liberal factor earlier, judicial

8 Cass R. Sunstein, *Designing Democracy: What Constitutions Do*, 2001, 56.

9 Cass R. Sunstein, *One Case at a Time: Judicial Minimalism on the Supreme Court*, 1999; Sunstein (note 6).

10 Cass R. Sunstein, *Radicals in Robes: Why Extreme Right-Wing Courts Are Wrong for America*, 2005; Cass R. Sunstein, Second-Order Perfectionism, 75 *Fordham L. Rev.* 2867 (2007).

minimalism may reach social peace by avoiding fundamental and controversial theorization in reasonable pluralism.

Certainly Sunstein notices several problems relating to stability which judicial minimalism would bring about.[11] The problems include inequality, unpredictability, reduction of transparency, and burdens on subsequent decision makers.[12] However, we must point out two other important problems which loom large before Sunstein's theory. First, in his *The Partial Constitution*, Sunstein endorses "a Republic of Reasons," where government must always have a reason for what it does.[13] Reason-giving is one of the most important conditions for the legitimacy of governance. Naked preferences are therefore strictly prohibited and status quo neutrality is severely challenged. Sunstein's position looks unchanged when he writes that "one of the points of constitutional arrangements is to protect the process of reason-giving, ensuring something like a 'republic of reasons.'"[14] How can minimalism be reconciled with the criticism against the status quo neutrality?

Minimalism has two kinds: Burkean and rational. Burkean minimalists are interested in established traditions, while rational minimalists are more focused on reasons behind long-standing practices. Burkean minimalists are less willing to subject practices to careful scrutiny.[15] Burkeans are skeptical of reason. Edmund Burke himself states that "they [men of speculation] think it more wise to continue the prejudice, with the reason involved, than to cast away the coat of prejudice, and to leave nothing but the naked reason."[16] Burkeans are rebels in a republic of reasons. Burkean minimalist judges may decide the case just by claiming that "this is our long-standing practice, period." Such judgments are inconsistent with the requirement of reason-giving.

One possible way to resolve the contradiction is to introduce the division of labor between lawmakers and judges: the role of the congress is to establish and justify new practices; the role of the court is to hold the practices. Judges are immune from the task of offering reasons and invoking principles. It is legislators that carry out the task. This understanding seems plausible when he emphasizes "an aspiration to *political* reason-giving" (emphasis added).[17] This is the point where deliberative democracy meets judicial minimalism. We shall return to this point later in Section 2-C.

The second problem concerning satiability Sunstein must deal with is that judicial minimalism fails to show mutual respect. This criticism might seem invalid because Sunstein himself emphasizes that incompletely theorized agree-

11 Sunstein (note 9); Cass R. Sunstein, Problems with Minimalism, 58 *Stanf. L. Rev.* 1899 (2006); Sunstein (note 2).
12 Sunstein (note 11), 1907.
13 Cass R. Sunstein, *The Partial Constitution*, 1993, ch. 1.
14 Sunstein (note 8), 239.
15 Sunstein (note 6), 356, 377.
16 Edmund Burke, *Reflections on the Revolution in France* (edited with an Introduction and Notes by L. G. Mitchell), 1790 [1993], 87.
17 Sunstein (note 1), 60.

ments enable people to show a measure of reciprocity. However, the point here is the quality of respect. Mutual respect in incompletely theorized agreements implies that we should not challenge our "fellow citizen's deepest and most defining commitments."[18] This kind of respect is superficial. Since we are not required to give them reasons for our conclusions, we do not treat them as rational agents. We defer to their strong convictions because they blindly devote themselves to their fallacious beliefs. We tolerate them because they are pitiful. This is just tolerance in a negative sense.[19] When judges take minimalism to avoid disagreements, they do not show sincere respect, not only to their co-judges but also to their fellow citizens. We fail to show reasonable respect to each other unless we try to grant justificatory reasons for our actions and decisions, even if we often disagree about what they really are.

B. Capacity

As discussed above, the notion of stability does not lead us to judicial minimalism. Judicial minimalism must thus rely on other considerations than social peace in pluralism. Sunstein mentions two of them: limited capacities of judges and deliberative democracy. We examine both in order.

The decisions of judges are usually incompletely theorized "because of limits of time and capacity". [20]Sunstein writes that "any approach for constitutional interpretation must pay close attention to the problem of judicial fallibility."[21] "Judges are not trained as philosophers, and judges who make theoretically ambitious arguments may well make mistakes that are quite costly."[22] Broad and abstract deep questions are hard for judges to handle.[23] Wide and deep rulings often invite errors.[24] Judicial minimalism is an effective method to cut error costs.

This argument does not, however, fit the ideal of deliberative democracy. Lawmakers and ordinary citizens are no less fallible than judges. We are only human. We are limited and bounded in time and capacity. Not only judges but also politicians often make erroneous judgments. The emphasis on bounded rationality brings about *political minimalism*: the democratic process must avoid wide and deep decisions and defer to long-standing traditions. Sunstein cannot help but accept not only judicial minimalism but also political minimalism. Political minimalism, however, compromises deliberation in democracy because the former allows us to skip the process of reason-giving; traditions are put beyond rational

18 Sunstein (note 2), 12.
19 Arthur Kaufmann, *Rechtsphilosophie*, 2 Ed., 1997, 329.
20 Sunstein (note 1), 50.
21 Sunstein (note 10), *Second-Order Perfectionism*, 2883.
22 Cass R. Sunstein From Theory to Practice, 29 *Arizona State Law Journal* 389 (1997), 400.
23 Sunstein (note 1), 49.
24 Sunstein (note 6), 362.

scrutiny. There is a sharp discrepancy between political minimalism and deliberative democracy.[25]

It would be helpful to distinguish between individual judges and the judiciary as a whole. Each judge has limited time and capacities. They are often not good at complete theorization of their decisions. However, the same applies to legislators and citizens. Individual limits of judges do not necessarily explain judicial minimalism. Rather, it would be better to understand that institutional limits of the judiciary defend judicial minimalism. Sunstein goes on this path when he emphasizes that "courts have serious institutional limits."[26] Two of them are relevant here. The first limit is on finding facts. Facts have been getting to play a more important role in understanding the law in our days.[27] For instance, it is necessary to investigate factual details to find the best rule for productive liability. Judges are ill-equipped with finding such a wide range of facts. The second limit is on effective social reform. Judicial decisions are often ineffective in bringing about social change because they lack the power to overcome resistance. *Brown v. Board of Education* brought about little desegregation. Real desegregation began only after the involvement of Congress and the Department of Justice in 1964.[28] The same holds true for *Roe v. Wade*. These institutional limits might probably explain judicial minimalism.

C. Democracy

However, it is important to notice that the institutional limits of courts do not necessarily justify judicial minimalism, because they may as well recommend us to restructure judicial institutions to give them more powerful resources. Rather, judicial minimalism follows from the proper role of the courts in constitutional arrangements. "Reliance on the courts may impair democratic channels for seeking changes, and in two ways. It might divert energy and resources from politics and the eventual judicial decision may foreclose a political outcome."[29] Courts are often referred as "the forum of principle," but Sunstein claims that the real forum of principle in the United States has been democratic rather than adjudica-

25 The same kind of problem arises in their new book *Nudge*. Richard H. Thaler and Cass R. Sunstein, *Nudge: Improving Decisions About Health, Wealth, and Happiness*, 2008. Thaler and Sunstein emphasize bounded rationality and therefore claim that it is important for planners to establish default rules that make people better off. Here we can find two different images of lawmakers: the one of limited capacity because he is also just a human and the one of extraordinary capacity because he is supposed to be omniscient and omnipotent so as to plan the best rules. It seems unstable and unclear how capable politicians are in Sunstein's theory.

26 Sunstein (note 13), 145.

27 Sunstein (note 22), 395.

28 Sunstein (note 13), 146; Sunstein (note 10), *Radicals in Robes*, 248.

29 Sunstein (note 13), 145.

tive.[30] Thus understood, the crucial reason for judicial minimalism is the ideal of deliberative democracy. Democracy is the third and decisive reason for judicial minimalism.

Sunstein's defense of judicial minimalism depends on the fact that judicial minimalism tends to inspire democratic debate.[31] Where judges make wide and deep rulings, deliberation in the congress will deteriorate. Judges' deference to legislators activates democratic deliberation. We raise two questions about this argument. First, it is an empirical question whether minimalism facilitates democratic debate. On the one hand, minimalist rulings sometimes have so little impact that they may not stir public deliberation. On the other hand, maximalist judgments often stimulate democratic processes. For instance, the Supreme Court of Japan ruled in 2005 that the public office election law was unconstitutional because it did not guarantee the right to vote for Japanese nationals living abroad, though two dissents out of fourteen judges defend minimalism by saying that the issue at stake should be deliberated and decided in the Diet. The ruling stimulated deliberation in the Diet and the law was revised in 2006. If the Supreme Court did not pronounce the law unconstitutional, public deliberation on that matter would not have stirred. It is uncertain whether the consideration of democracy-promoting supports judicial minimalism.

Second, it is unclear why Sunstein supports deliberative democracy. On the one hand, he says the ideal of self-government is significant in itself.[32] Deliberative democracy is thus justified in deontological terms. On the other hand, he sometimes suggests that deliberative democracy produces better consequences. When he analyzes "deliberative trouble" such as cascades and group polarization, he supposes that it is a problem because it results in worse outcomes.[33] Deliberative democracy is here defended in terms of consequentialism. The crucial question is this: When deliberation produces worse consequences, does Sunstein still support deliberative democracy? Or, does he claim that deliberative democracy never results in bad outcomes? We will return to this question in Section 3-C.

3. Sunstein's Whole Theory of Law

So far we have discussed three grounds for judicial minimalism: stability, limited capacity, and deliberative democracy. We have shown that it is the decisive reason for judicial minimalism to promote deliberation in democratic arenas. Now let us turn to Sunstein's whole jurisprudence including judicial minimalism.

30 Sunstein (note 1), 60.
31 Sunstein (note 9), ch. 2.
32 Sunstein (note 2), 15; Sunstein (note 10), *Radicals in Robes*, 247.
33 Sunstein (note 8), ch. 1. When he emphasizes the importance of dissent, he says "unchecked by dissent, conformity can produce disturbing, harmful, and sometimes astonishing *outcomes*" Cass R. Sunstein, *Why Societies Need Dissent*, 2003 (emphasis added).

A. First-Order Minimalism

Sunstein cautiously remarks that there are problems with judicial minimalism.[34] Judges may not always follow a minimalist approach, but must choose between wide and narrow judgments. They must examine "which is best, all things considered."[35] The choice between narrow and wide rulings cannot itself be resolved by rule; it must be made on a case-by-case basis.[36] There is no justification for a general presumption in favor of minimalism.[37]

As we have seen, judges sometimes blunder because of limits of time and capacities. In order to reduce the costs of errors, minimalists favor narrowness. Hard minimalists stick to narrowness. Sunstein is not a hard minimalist; he is a soft minimalist. He admits that minimalism is not the best theory in every possible world,[38] and that originalism or perfectionism makes sense in some times and places.[39] Soft minimalism, however, may invite not only those errors resulting from wide judgments, the first order errors, but also those resulting from the meta-level judgments, the second order errors. Soft minimalism thus ends in losing the merits of minimalism.

B. Second-Order Perfectionism

Despite the fact of increasing error costs, Sunstein supports soft minimalism instead of hard minimalism because minimalism is best understood as a kind of second-order perfectionism. Perfectionism holds the view that "the Constitution should be construed in a way that makes it best, and in that sense perfects it."[40] Ronald Dworkin is the most powerful champion of perfectionism. Sunstein asserts minimalism rather than perfectionism on the first-order, but defends perfectionism on the second-order.

Sunstein emphasizes that no theory of interpretation of law makes sense in every possible world. Several conditions make minimalism more plausible than other approaches such as originalism, perfectionism, and majoritarianism. He points out the three conditions to be met: (1) originalism would produce bad results; (2) long-standing traditions and practices are trustworthy; (3) judges lack enough theory-building capacities.[41] Reversely put, where these conditions are not met, minimalism is less plausible. Since Sunstein believes that some areas of current legal traditions in the United States meet the conditions, he concludes

34 Sunstein (note 2); Sunstein (note 11).
35 Sunstein (note 11), 1912.
36 Sunstein (note 11), 1917.
37 Sunstein (note 11), 1910.
38 Sunstein (note 6), 360, 386; Sunstein (note 9), 262.
39 Sunstein (note 10), *Radicals in Robes*, 246.
40 Sunstein (note 10), *Second-Order Perfectionism*, 2868.
41 Sunstein (note 6), 361.

that Burkean minimalism is the best approach to those areas of American constitutional law, though, he admits that Burkean minimalism is not consistent with entrenched understandings in other domains like the Equal Protection Clause.[42] Thus, Sunstein's whole theory of law includes not only judicial minimalism but also other approaches with the conditions to be met in order to adopt one over others. The title "beyond judicial minimalism" suggests this understanding of his theory. Judicial minimalism is only the tip of the iceberg; the rest is below the sea.

Thus understood, the important point is what those conditions are. When should a judge take an approach to law, and when another? What conditions make an approach better than others? The demarcation of domains of the law becomes one of the main tasks for judges. How should judges answer the demarcation question? Here comes perfectionism: an approach that makes legal material "the best it can be."[43] Sunstein endorses minimalism as the first order theory in some domains of American constitutional law while he accepts perfectionism as the second order theory of interpretation of law when he claims "Burkean minimalism can be understood as a kind of second-order perfectionism – that is, a form of perfectionism that is alert to the institutional weaknesses of the federal judiciary, and that therefore refuses to pursue perfectionism directly."[44] Sunstein thus admits that judges must refer to perfectionism when they give an answer to a demarcation question.

C. Third-Order Pragmatism

Sunstein then adds that "second-order perfectionism is, in fact, a good understanding of the *pragmatic* nature of Burkean minimalism" (emphasis added).[45] In what sense is perfectionism pragmatic? Interpretation, as Dworkin analyzes, consists of the two dimensions: fit and justification. Following Dworkin's understanding, Sunstein argues that Burkean minimalism both fits and justifies our practices. The elements of fit and justification do not straightly lead us to the pragmatic position because we can justify an action on non-pragmatic considerations such as contractualism or Kantianism. Instead of Kantianism, Sunstein basically relies on consequentialism in order to justify minimalism: "respect for traditions is likely to produce better results"[46] than other approaches. He explains Burkean minimalism by saying that "the basic idea is that if courts follow traditions, they will produce better consequences, all things considered, than they might under any other approach to interpretation."[47] Therefore, Burkeanism can be best under-

42 Sunstein (note 6), 400.
43 Ronald Dworkin, *Law's Empire*, 1986, 226.
44 Sunstein (note 6), 395.
45 Sunstein (note 6), 395.
46 Sunstein (note 6), 359.
47 Sunstein (note 6), 359.

stood in pragmatic or consequentialist terms, or "as a way of promoting utility or at least good consequences --- if only indirectly."[48] What is then the relationship between perfectionism, which he claims is the appropriate interpretive method of law, and pragmatism, which underlies Sunstein's whole jurisprudence? We might probably understand his theory as the third-order pragmatism – that is a form of pragmatism which justifies perfectionist interpretation as the means to promote better results. Minimalism just operates as a kind of heuristic approach to produce better consequences.

Pragmatism or consequentialism pervades Sunstein's whole jurisprudence. For example, when Sunstein considers how to specify minimalism's domain, he suggests the criterion of whether the relevant tradition reflects "the independent judgments of many people."[49] This is, at best, confusing, because the independence of judgments does not seem intrinsic to minimalism. Consequentialist character could, however, explain his suggestion that Condorcet Jury Theorem requires the independence of many people's judgments to affirm the correctness of the verdict. Thus understood, Sunstein thoroughly endorses pragmatism or consequentialism as the third order theory.

Thus, Sunstein's theory of law consists of first-order minimalism, second-order perfectionism, and third-order pragmatism. Table 1 helps clarify the status of Sunstein's jurisprudence in relation to other approaches.

Table 1

1st order	**Interpretive Method for Judges**	**minimalism**, maximalism, perfectionism, originalism, majoritarianism
2nd order	**Nature of Interpretation**	**perfectionism**, positivism (or conventionalism)
3rd order	**Basic Value**	equality, autonomy, efficiency, **better consequences (or pragmatic concern)**

(Sunstein's positions are shown in bold)

The first order is about the question "Which interpretive method should judges take?" Sunstein defends minimalism, rejects originalism, and criticizes originalism and majoritarianism. The second order concerns the question "What is the nature of interpretation?" Sunstein accepts perfectionism: interpretation consists of fit and justification and interpretation of law is to make legal material the best it can be. He does not take positivism or conventionalism, which say that interpretation of law is to find what the law is as it is declared. The third order bears on the question "What is the basic value which justifies legal practices?" Sunstein does not go

48 Sunstein (note 6), 360.
49 Sunstein (note 6), 405.

along with Dworkin (equal concern) and James E. Fleming (deliberative autonomy),[50] but adopts pragmatism or consequentialism.

Let us compare Sunstein and Dworkin to make clear the similarities and differences between them. On the one hand, they share perfectionism at the second stage. They agree that interpretation of law is to show legal practices in the best light. On the other hand, they disagree at the first and third stages. While Dworkin claims that judges should adopt perfectionism at the first stage, as Hercules does, Sunstein says that they should take minimalism at the first stage in order to achieve the second-order perfection. They also differ at the third stage. Dworkin regards integrity as an intrinsic value to law; integrity is best understood in reference to equality.[51] Dworkin argues that it is essential to the idea of law that we are governed by the principles which treat us as equals.[52] As contrasted with Dworkin, Sunstein defends pragmatism: an interpretation of law is right if and only if it results in better consequences.[53] Briefly put, the main differences between them lie in the role of judges in a democratic society and their fundamental value in jurisprudence.

D. Division of Labor

We have examined where Sunstein is heading towards beyond judicial minimalism. To conclude this comment, let us ask the final question: "What is he?" Despite the emphasis on the importance of incompletely theorized agreements, Sunstein himself vigorously defends his theory of law and has a great ambition to build a complete theory of constitutional law. We might find a kind of performative inconsistency in Sunstein's works. I understand that he implicitly suggests that it is appropriate to divide the social roles between judges and legal theorists. Judges are officially expected to make a judgment on a case on hand, while legal scholars are not required to decide a case in real time. Legal scholars' opinions do not (fortunately?) affect the people so much as judges. Legal scholars usually have more time than judges to elaborate a theory of law. The court produces legal materials; the law school enriches them by giving them a theoretical account. This division of labor between judges and legal theorists might explain the different approaches Sunstein adopts at the first and the second stages. Minimalism is the best approach for judges; perfectionism is the appropriate approach for legal scholars. Perfectionism by legal scholars might avoid those problems perfection-

50 James E. Fleming, The Incredible Shrinking Constitutional Theory: From the Partial Constitution to the Minimal Constitution, 75 *Fordham L. Rev.* 2885 (2007).

51 Dworkin (note 43).

52 Ronald Dworkin, *Justice in Robes*, 2006, 73.

53 If it is correct that Sunstein deeply accepts pragmatism as we have discussed, it will follow that his defense of deliberative democracy relies on pragmatic concerns. *See* Section 2-C.

ism by judges (that is, judicial perfectionism) would invite: social instability, limited time, and democratic impairment.

It remains to be explained why judges should accept a legal theorist's suggestion that minimalism perfects constitutional practice. It would be better to suppose that judges are responsible for the second-order judgments as well as the first-order decisions. This is the question Dworkin posed to Sunstein,[54] and I agree with Dworkin. Despite disagreements about judges' responsibility, we can agree that the task of legal scholars is to completely theorize legal judgments. This comment is a small step toward such theorization.

Hirohide Takikawa
College of Law and Politics
Rikkyo University
Tokyo, Japan

54 Dworkin (note 53), 66.

Hidetomi Omori, Okayama, Japan

Can minimalism make the judiciary and the legislature cooperate?

Comment on Cass R. Sunstein, Beyond Judicial Minimalism, in: *Judicial Minimalism: For and Against,* Ninth Kobe Lecture, Aoyama Gakuin University, Tokyo, Japan, June 7, 2008.

My comment tries to examine the limits of minimalism focusing on the assumptions of the institutional roles of different branches of government. It is divided into two parts. The first part is designed to make clear the assumptions of minimalism, that is, how minimalism understands the institutional roles of the judiciary and the legislature. The second part is designed to examine critically whether the minimalist way of interpretation can adequately promote the cooperation between them.

First, I would like to begin with laying out the assumptions of minimalism: its understanding of the institutional roles of the judiciary and the legislature.

Minimalism itself is a theory of interpretation that requires judges to issue narrow and shallow rulings. But it seems to depend on an assumption of the institutional roles of different branches of government. It may be taken as the synthesis of what I call "judiciary-degrading" and "legislature-admiring."

By "judiciary-degrading," I mean that minimalism underestimates the institutional ability of the judiciary. It requires judges to issue narrow and shallow rulings because it must assume that they do not have the competence for the following two tasks. First, they cannot decide many cases with one general rule because they do not have enough information about the future. They do not know what will occur afterwards. They tend to avoid increasing the decision cost and error cost. [1]Therefore, minimalism prefers narrow rulings to broad ones. Second, they cannot reach a consensus on contentious moral problems on which many views conflict, because they do not have enough knowledge or experience to resolve large-scale problems of the right or the good. They are neither philosophers nor priests. They tend to resolve problems through incompletely theorized agreement.[2] So, minimalism favors shallow rulings, not deep ones.

By "legislature-admiring," on the other hand, I mean that the legislature is the most adequate arena for democratic self-government. This thesis seems a corollary of the former "judiciary-degrading" thesis, or another side of the same coin. The court is underestimated, so the assembly is highly appraised. It is surprising that minimalism eloquently emphasizes the inabilities of the court, whereas it tells us

1 Cass R. Sunstein, *One Case At A Time: Judicial Minimalism on the Supreme Court,* 1999, 50.
2 Cass R. Sunstein, *Legal Reasoning and Political Conflict*, 1996, 45.

little about the defects of the assembly. It is not clear how highly it appraises the competence of the assembly, but it cannot be denied that it depends on a confidence in the legislature. If not, it claims only that judges should abandon their responsibilities as decision-makers by requiring them to avoid broad and deep decisions. There underlies the theory, it seems, an expectation that the assembly can resolve controversial questions through democratic deliberation in place of the court.[3] This may be derived from liberal republicanism that "will attempt to promote deliberation among multiple voices in the political process,"[4] as Professor Sunstein has claimed elsewhere.

These two theories of institutional roles, which are inextricably linked, seem to uphold the minimalist way of interpretation. In brief, they seem to claim that because the court cannot resolve large-scale issues at a deep level, it should avoid judging them and refer them instead to the assembly.

Now I would like to embark on the next step, to examine whether the minimalist way of interpretation based on these theses can succeed in promoting the cooperation between the judiciary and the legislature. Can narrow and shallow rulings make these branches function well? Overall, I conclude the following, broken into three points.

First, narrow and shallow rulings may reduce the decision costs and error costs in the court, but increase them in the assembly. In other words, they only export these costs from the court to other branches, including the later courts or the assembly. But this "export" strategy is not desirable in the overall system of decision-making, which is composed of the different branches of government. At any rate, the issues must be resolved somewhere. If the court refers the resolutions to other branches of government, it abandons responsibilities that might sometimes be expected for continuing law-making. Certainly, Professor Sunstein is very conscious of this point. He says, "narrow rulings will impose significant decision-making burdens on others – and very possibly increase decision costs on balance,"[5] and "[t]here is no justification for a general presumption in favor of standards or narrowness."[6] This is indisputable. However, in order to require judges to issue narrow and shallow rulings, it is necessary to validate in advance the following two points. One is that it is more efficient to export those costs in an overall system of decision-making; there are other branches that can deal more efficiently

3 Certainly, Professor Sunstein admits that the main stage of deliberative democracy, where the large-scale issues are debated, "is in democratic processes, not in courtrooms." Sunstein (note 2), 195. *See also* Cass R. Sunstein, Burkean Minimalism, 105 *Mich. L. Rev.* 303 (2006), 383-84. But he also said that in some cases, in which some groups face barriers to exercising political influence, the court should not adopt the attitude of deference to the legislature. *See*, Cass R. Sunstein, *The Partial Constitution*, 1993, 142-43.

4 Cass R. Sunstein, Beyond the Republican Revival, 97 *Yale L. J.* 1539 (1988), 1571.

5 Cass R. Sunstein, Beyond Judicial Minimalism, in: *Judicial Minimalism: For and Against*, Ninth Kobe Lecture, Aoyama Gakuin University, Tokyo, Japan, 2008, 15.

6 Sunstein (note 5), 17; *See also*, Sunstein (note 1), 4-5, 21. 40-, 53-4, Cass R. Sunstein, Problems of Minimalism, 58 *Stan. L. R.* 1899 (2006), 1909.

with those costs than the court. Another is that if a specific branch of government is to be identified as the assembly, it is better at dealing with those costs; making more accurate decisions and making fewer errors. But unfortunately these do not seem to be convincingly demonstrated.

Second, narrow and shallow rulings may create conflicts in the assembly, even though there might be agreements in the court. That is, in heterogeneous societies, if the court avoids general and deep judgments, people may dispute the decisions intensely and their representatives may also contest them in the assembly. Consider the case of abortion which is a controversial moral question confronted by pro-choice and pro-life advocates. Professor Sunstein shows *Roe v. Wade* as a successful example where judges may agree in spite of their diverse reasoning.[7] Putting aside the question of the *Roe* case as a successful example for minimalism,[8] even if the *Roe* case was agreed by judges despite their diverse reasoning, it would never resolve the underlying question about the morals of abortion. In fact, the conflicts regarding abortion would continue afterwards. For example, in the state of South Dakota, in response to the *Roe* case, a bill banning abortion was discussed and passed in the state legislature (later repealed by a narrow margin by referendum). And, as is pointed out, other states would follow South Dakota. Whether the bills banning abortion are passed or not, it is anticipated that the conflicts on abortion will continue in spite of the *Roe* case. We have good reasons to believe that they will even intensify because the assembly is more sensitive to or more reflected by diverse opinions of many people, including pro-choice and pro-life advocates.

Third, narrow and shallow rulings may impede, not promote, democratic self-government through the assembly. They may rather be harmful to deliberative democracy. Professor Sunstein says "narrow rules preserve a great deal of space for continuing discussion and debate."[9] If people or their representatives discuss the questions on which the court has not judged, it may serve the idea of self-government. But, however large a space the court preserves, the assembly will not necessarily try to discuss the questions on which the court has not judged. The essential point is that the court's decision does not necessarily bind the conduct of the assembly. Even if the court issued narrow rulings and preserved a large space for discussion, the assembly will get the scope or opportunity, but not the reason or duty, to legislate.

Furthermore, if the assembly is not functioning well as an arena of deliberative democracy, narrow and shallow rulings may make us lose self-government. In

7 Sunstein (note 5), 5.

8 In order to understand how Professor Sunstein evaluates the *Roe* case itself, *see*, Sunstein (note 2), 180, Sunstein (note 1), 17-18, Cass R. Sunstein, *Radicals in Robes: Why Extreme Right-Wing Courts Are Wrong for America*, 2005, 248-49, and Sunstein (note 3), Burkean Minimilism, 403. *See also*, Antonin Scalia (Foreword), *Originalism: A Quarter-Century of Debate* (ed. By Steven G. Calabresi) , 2007, 294, 311.

9 Sunstein (note 5), 15.

the actual assemblies, representatives often depend on inclinations of various interest groups and tend to make compromises and adjustments of their particular interests.[10] In this case, the assemblies serve to aggregate private interests, not to make public decisions. If the court issued a narrow and shallow ruling in this situation, they would strengthen this tendency. If the assembly functions well as an arena for deliberative democracy, they might serve self-government, but if not, they would help to maintain the status quo in the political process.

These three points which I have identified seem to be derived from the synthesis of "judiciary-degrading" and "legislature-admiring." They suggest that minimalism cannot adequately promote the cooperation between the judiciary and the legislature. If that is the case, the court has to issue more positive – less narrow and shallow – rulings than minimalism requires. We might well go far beyond minimalism – maybe further than Professor Sunstein admits.

Hidetomi Omori
Graduate School of Humanities and Social Sciences
Okayama University
Okayama, Japan

10 Professor Sunstein seems to admit that the actual assemblies do not function well as an arena of deliberative democracy. *See* Sunstein (note 4), 1549-50.

Yoh Matsuo [*], Osaka, Japan

"Putting Judicial Minimalism into the Context of the American Constitutional Theory"

Comment on Cass R. Sunstein, Beyond Judicial Minimalism, in: *Judicial Minimalism: For and Against,* Ninth Kobe Lecture, Aoyama Gakuin University, Tokyo, Japan, June 7, 2008

1. Putting judicial minimalism into the context of American Constitutional theory
2. Meaning of "Incompletely Theorized Agreement"
3. Hidden assumptions of Judicial Minimalism: Beyond the "Rehnquist Court" paradigm to Popular Constitutionalism?

Introduction

I will try to put judicial minimalism into context and then describe the meanings and limits of judicial minimalism. My comment consists of three parts. Part I will try to make clear what forms of judicial restraint judicial minimalism is by comparing it with Bickel's "passive virtues," and then will try to describe judicial minimalism as a form of anti-"Warren Court" paradigm. Part II will compare the incomplete theorization strategy with the reason-giving strategy and then show the significance of incomplete theorization. Part III will demonstrate hidden assumptions of judicial minimalism by comparing it with recent developments in American Constitutional theory.

1. What is Judicial Minimalism?

A. Judicial Restraint: Alexander Bickel's Form and Cass Sunstein's Form

Cass Sunstein's judicial minimalism can be understood as a kind of judicial restraint. My aim here is to understand how courts use restraint in judicial minimalism by comparing it with Alexander Bickel's theory, and to explore its significance in American Constitutional theory.

Alexander Bickel is among those arguing for judicial restraint in post-war periods. But his theory of judicial restraint is different from Sunstein's. Bickel's judicial restraint starts from maintaining "the principled process of enunciating and

* Research for this article was supported by Scientific Research Grant – Academic Generative Research Expense, "New Ordering of Market and Society in Post-Structural Reform: Legal System for Freedom and Community."

applying certain enduring values of our society,"[1] for which Herbert Wechsler argued. Unlike Wechsler, Bickel understood the tension between principle and expediency, which he called "the Lincolnian tension," and exaggerated the importance of the court's "third" power neither to strike down legislation as inconsistent with principle nor to legitimate legislation as consistent with principle, that is, a power to stay its hand ("passive virtues") in order not only to maintain "the principled process" in courts but also to make possible a principled government.[2] The aim of Bickel's judicial restraint is to maintain "the principled process" within courts and then focus on justiciability.

Cass Sunstein also aims to work out a principled government, "a Republic of Reasons."[3] But unlike Bickel, he does not think that "the principled process" should be in the courts. Sunstein's main purpose is to revive (or to believe in?) the possibilities of democratic politics.[4] But he requires that democratic politics not be expedient but principled. He takes a principled democracy as deliberative. While "the principled process" should lie in the courts in Bickel's judicial restraint, it should be in democratic politics according to Sunstein's theory. So what a role do courts play in the deliberative democracy? Sunstein's judicial minimalism urges courts to make decisions by avoiding "broad rulings and theoretical ambition,"[5] that is, incompletely theorized agreements, so that it can constrain to some extent "the principled process" in the courts; for courts to leave things undecided can promotes deliberation.

Bickel and Sunstein have a common purpose, but different views of the court's role and different strategies in the court's decision-making.

	Passive virtues	Judicial Minimalism
Main purpose	Principled government	Deliberative democracy
Courts' role	Judicial prudence or avoiding expediency in courts	Democracy-promoting, avoidance of political costs, etc.
Form	Staying one's hands	Avoiding broad rulings and theoretical ambition

B. Judicial Minimalism as an Anti-"Warren Court" Paradigm

In American Constitutional theory, especially since the Warren court era, the view that the Court, engaged in principled reasoning or giving reasons for the judicial process, was "the forum of principle," while the political process was the forum

1 A. Bickel, *The Least Dangerous Branch*, 1962, 58.
2 Bickel (note 1), 65-72.
3 Cass R. Sunstein, *The Partial Constitution*, 1998.
4 Sunstein (note 3), 146.
5 Cass R. Sustein, Beyond Judicial Minimalism, in: *Judicial Minimalism: For and Against*, Ninth Kobe Lecture, 2008. 1.

for unprincipled compromises, so influencing Japanese legal philosophy and constitutional theory[6], and we call this view the "Warren Court" paradigm.

This "Warren Court" paradigm has been criticized by several critics, and we call the critiques anti-"Warren Court" paradigm, which involves originalism and popular constitutionalism. Judicial minimalism can also be understood as one form of the anti-"Warren Court" paradigm, because it aims to revive democratic politics by constraining principled reasoning in the courts. Judicial minimalism is different from originalism (or fundamentalism) which urges the Court to rely on original intent for constitutional interpretation in not doing much more than is necessary to resolve cases[7], and from popular constitutionalism in supporting judicial supremacy. The latter difference will be examined later.

2. Meaning of "Incompletely Theorized Agreement"

As noted above, judicial minimalism is an incomplete theorization strategy[8] rather than reason-giving by courts.[9] But what is reason-giving?

Fredrick Schauer analyzes the logical structure of a reason and makes clear the significance of reason-giving.[10] He shows that "to provide a reason for a decision is to include the decision within a principle of greater generality than the decision itself," that giving reasons has "the decision-disciplining function," and that giving reasons may be a sign of respect.[11] By comparing these three features of reason-giving with incomplete theorized agreements, we will see what incomplete theorization means.

6 For example, Kōji Sato, one of the most prominent professors in constitutional law in Japan, takes judicial branch as "a forum of principle (hō-genri-kikan)" and this view is held by Tatsuo Inoue, one of the most prominent professors in legal philosophy in Japan. But they do not seem to take legislation as only unprincipled process.

7 So, judicial minimalism does not need to take sides on particular methods of constitutional interpretation such as originalism and integrity. Therefore, judicial minimalism can also be understood as a meta-method of constitutional interpretation, that is, a method by which several judges disagreeing on methods of constitutional interpretation can come to agree on particular outcomes. This understanding of judicial minimalism does not necessarily encourage judges to reason by analogy.

8 The term 'strategy' means that incomplete theorization depends on situations.

9 In Sunstein (note 5), Professor Sunstein said that judicial minimalism did not deny reason-giving by courts. Indeed, incomplete theorization involves theorization and does not cast away reason-giving. But it constrains reason-giving by courts to the extent that it can promote democratic deliberation and mutual respect.

10 Frederick Schauer, Giving Reasons, 47 Stanford Law Review, 633 (1995)

11 Schauer (note 10).

A. Generality, Two Forms of Stability, and Impartiality

Cass Sunstein describes incomplete theorization as wary of the reason-giving strategy because of its over- and under-inclusiveness.[12] As Schauer admits,[13] generality can be over- and under-inclusive. Schauer grounds generality (or "ruleness") on the formal stability which narrows the range of potential decisions in the future different from the political stability in which there are less troubles even when people disagree on first principles. Sunstein claims that incomplete theorization can reduce the political costs of enduring disagreements.[14] Incomplete theorization can be thought to be based on political stability.[15] Here two questions arise. First if formal stability can trade off political stability,[16] which stability should we choose for what reason? Second, is promoting stability, formal or political, consistent with the principle of impartiality which "requires government to provide reasons that can be intelligible to different people from different premises"[17] and if so, when?

B. Disciplining who or what?

Frederick Schauer explores the possibility that giving reasons can discipline decision-makers to improve their quality of decisions.[18] His arguments are simple: giving reasons ensures generality (particular decisions are often the result of decision-maker's partiality) and generality is likely to exclude the decision-maker's partiality. So giving reasons for a decision is likely to discipline decision-makers.

By contrast, incomplete theorization, or leaving things undecided, can promote deliberation in other branches or citizens. In this case, the object to discipline is someone other than the decision-maker. Sunstein's arguments are also simple: incompleteness shows disagreement, disagreement is a necessary condition of deliberation,[19] and incompleteness can promote deliberation.[20] Incom-

12 Cass R. Sunstein, Incompletely Theorized Agreements, 108 *Harv. L. Rev.* 1733 (1995), 1755.

13 Frederick Schauer, *Playing by the Rules; A Philosophical Examination of Rule-Based Decision-Making in Law and in Life*, 1991, 31-34.

14 Sunstein (note 5), 12.

15 Sunstein (note 5), 11-12 (Sunstein understands stability as "social stability.").

16 *See* Schauer (note 10), 156 (Stability by rules (formal stability) may very well turn out to be politically or psychologically destabilizing, because formal stability often creates pressure for radical change).

17 Sunstein (note 3), 24.

18 Schauer (note 10), 653.

19 Sunstein (note 5), 19 (Interestingly, Sunstein says that agreements may be a product of coercion or of a failure of imagination). Indeed, disagreement can excite people's imagination. But is imagination more likely to be excited in politically unstable society than in politically stable society?

20 Sunstein (note 3), 24; Cass R. Sunstein, *One Case at a Time: Judicial Minimalism on the Supreme Court*, 1999; and Sunstein (note 5).

plete theorized agreements try to discipline someone other than those who make agreements. For example, incomplete theorization in courts decisions can promote deliberation in legislatures.

Indeed, incompletely theorized agreements in one branch leave things undecided in another branch. But it does not ensure impartiality in the other branch.[21] Incomplete theorization may be a necessary condition for deliberation but not a sufficient condition. And if Schauer's analysis is right, should courts encourage the other branches to give reasons for their decisions?[22]

C. Two Views of Respect

While Schauer suggests that giving reasons may be a sign of respect, Sunstein claims that incomplete theorized agreements can enable people to show each other a measure of mutual respect.[23] Where does this difference come from?

I think it comes from two views of respect for others.[24] One view is that people respect each other when they dialogue without showing each other their own moral and religious belief. Incomplete theorized agreements show each other this type of respect. The other view is that people respect each other when they show each other their own moral and religious belief and learn from each other. Giving reasons shows each other this type of respect.

But Sunstein seems to employ the latter view when he discusses deliberative democracy.[25] Can deliberative democracy be consistent with incomplete theorized agreements?

Giving Reasons vs. Incomplete Theorization

	Giving reasons	Incomplete theorization
Logical structure	Generalization	Particularity (not full)
Disciplining what?	Decision-maker (courts)	Someone other than the courts (legislation)
Forms of respect	Showing one's own belief	Hiding one's own belief

21 Institutionalization of impartiality, *see* Adrian Vermeule, *Mechanisms of Democracy: Institutional Design Writ Small*, 2007.
22 Sunstein (note 3) (Sunstein once urged courts to do this. But can judicial minimalism be consistent with that suggestion?)
23 Sunstein (note 5). 12.
24 For two views of respect, see Ryōsuke Hirai, *Taiwa no seigi: taiwateki-seigiron to democrashii no kanōsei* [Justice of Dialogue: Theory of Dialogic Justice and Possibilities of Democracy]," in: *Seigi: gendaishakai no kōkyōtetsugaku wo motomete [Justice: In Search of Public Philosophy in Modern Society]*, ed. Ryōsuke Hirai, 2004.
25 Sunstein (note 20), *One Case at a Time: Judicial Minimalism on the Supreme Court*, 24-25 ("But in a deliberative democracy, a premium is also placed on the exchange of reasons by people with different information and diverse perspectives.").

3. Another Way?: Beyond the "Rehnquist Court" paradigm to Popular Constitutionalism or Legislative Supremacy

Recently in American Constitutional theory, departmentalism has been supported as an alternative to judicial supremacy, which "consists of the ability of the Supreme Court to erase the distinction between its own opinions interpreting the Constitution and the actual Constitution itself."[26] Judicial supremacy has been strongly supported by the Rehnquist Court.[27] Departmentalism, which was Thomas Jefferson's view, denies this judicial supremacy and claims that each branch of government has an equal authority and responsibility to interpret the Constitution.[28]

As noted above, one of the arguments in judicial minimalism is the avoidance of political costs of enduring disagreements. But if we accept departmentalism and deny judicial supremacy, the political costs of disagreements would be lower, because losers in particular cases lose only in that case and disagreements would not be less enduring than by not accepting departmentalism. Even if the supreme court decides by complete theorization, other branches need not surrender to that judgment. But if Sunstein does not take this theory and deny judicial supremacy, why not? Then, do we not come to the time to reconsider judicial supremacy?

Or judicial minimalism can take another form, that is, legislative supremacy (or parliamentary sovereignty). What does Sunstein think of this theory?

Yoh Matsuo
Faculty of Law
Kinki University
Osaka, Japan

26 *See* Keith E. Whittington, P*olitical Foundations of Judicial Supremacy: The Presidency, the Supreme Court and Constitutional Leadership in U.S. History*, 2007, xi.

27 For discussions about judicial supremacy in the Rehnquist Court, *see* Mark Tushnet, *The New Constitutional Order*, 2003, 90-93.

28 *See* Larry D. Kramer, *The People Themselves: Popular Constitutionalism and Judicial Review*, 2004.

Hiroshi Kamemoto, Kyoto, Japan

Responsibility of the Planner

Comment on Cass R. Sunstein & Richard H. Thaler, Libertarian Paternalism Is Not an Oxymoron, 70 *U. Chi. L. Rev.* 1159 (2003)

Professor Cass R. Sunstein[1] puts forward a remarkable idea of institution planning which aims at both promoting welfare of people and respecting their freedom of choice by such means as appropriate default rules, starting points and framing for choice. Using stirring rhetoric, he calls it libertarian paternalism, for it combines freedom of choice (from libertarianism) and the welfare of others perspective (from paternalism). Bounded rationality and self-control of ordinary people underlie his arguments. He emphasizes that more complete planning requires much more empirical study.

I have little doubt about his main idea. I agree with him that it is good to facilitate choice through the offer of properly qualified options for the benefit of people in general. My concern is not with what he discussed but about what he refrained from discussing in his essay. This is the issue of the responsibility of the planner for the institution within which individuals make a choice. One of the most striking of Sunstein's statements is that 'the planners are human, and thus are both boundedly rational and subject to the influence of objectionable pressures'. Libertarians would think that this is one of the reasons why government officials are less trustworthy than private actors. But he puts it as a response to a libertarian objection to the paternalism of government. The point of such a criticism seems to be not that government planners are not subject to market pressures, as he seems to concede, but that they do not assume responsibility for the outcomes of their plans.

Individual citizens alone are supposed to be responsible for their choices among options offered by the planner, while her design in fact influences their behavior. Freedom of choice functions here not only for individuals to avoid unsuitable default plans, but also to justify individual responsibility and the planner's immunity. Libertarianism or liberalism in general, of course, implies the principle of self-responsibility: that a person cannot complain of the results from her own choice, even if they were bad. But if her available options are not ones that present themselves naturally but controlled by another, and if the results are worse than she expected, is she not entitled at least morally, apart from politically

1 Cass R. Sunstein and Richard H. Thaler, "Libertarian Paternalism Is Not an Oxymoron," *The University of Chicago Law Review*, vol.70. no.4, 1159-1202. Professor Sunstein delivered a lecture on this article at Kyoto Seminar in Kyoto University held in June 9th ,2008. I refer to Sunstein only, though the original article has a co-author. This short article represents my comments on his lecture at that time.

and legally, to complain, even if the planner had intended in good faith to promote welfare?

This is my question about libertarian paternalism. I do not have any definite answer. I add, however, that it would be unfair to ascribe bad outcomes to the planner, ascribing good outcomes to the individual alone[2] and not to the planner. The following matters should be considered. Who is responsible, how much and for what? How is the responsibility divided between the planner and the citizen? How should the responsibility for bad and good results be apportioned? The problem of responsibility for outcomes caused by individual behavior in the context of libertarian paternalism seems to exceed the theme of libertarian paternalism.

Hiroshi Kamemoto
Graduate School of Law
Kyoto University
Kyoto, Japan

2 I was struck by this important fact when I was reading R. H. Coase's *Essays on Economics and Economists*, Chicago and London, University of Chicago Press, 1994, at 59. He cites George J. Stigler, "The Formation of Economic Policy," in *Current Problems in Political Economy*, Ind., DePauw University, 74-75. He points out the problem of the policy that a physician may not be penalized when she belatedly uses a drug whose full effects we already know, but penalized when she uses too early one whose full effects are as yet not known. This is despite the fact that at least some number of otherwise dead patients could have survived, had she decided to use the new drug early and after serious consideration. Such a policy only takes account of bad outcomes, while good outcomes are ignored.

Susumu Morimura, Tokyo, Japan

"Libertarian Paternalism"

Comment on Cass R. Sunstein and Richard H. Thaler, Libertarian Paternalism Is Not an Oxymoron, 70 *U. Chi. L. Rev.* 1159 (2003)

1. Sunstein and Thaler's "Libertarian Paternalism" is not genuinely paternalistic

My first question concerning "Libertarian Paternalism Is Not an Oxymoron"[1] by Professors Sunstein and Thaler is: "Is their 'libertarian paternalism' paternalistic in the ordinary sense?" Sunstein and Thaler claim that the idea that "paternalism always involves coercion" is a misconception.[2] Indeed, I have been guilty of this misconception for many years and remain unrepentant.

I can call two renowned authors on paternalism in my defense. First, Joel Feinberg, the author of the four-volume magnum opus *The Moral Limits of the Criminal Law*, defines "legal paternalism" as the principle that "[i]t is always a good reason in support of a prohibition that it is necessary to prevent harm (physical, psychological, or economic) to the actor himself."[3] I understand that Feinberg's concept of prohibition includes coercion, but not mere discouragement or default rules. Next, *On Liberty* by John Stuart Mill is usually regarded as a passionate classic tract against paternalism. However, Mill not only permits, but also recommends "remonstrating with him [the actor], or reasoning with him, or persuading him, or entreating him"[4] for his own good. Sunstein and Thaler characterize their approach as paternalistic only because their "planners are not trying to track people's anticipated choice, but are self-consciously attempting to move people in welfare-promoting directions."[5] I do not think Mill would find Sunstein and Thaler's proposals incompatible with his Harm Principle. Then, even Mill's *On Liberty* would be paternalistic in Sunstein and Thaler's sense. They define paternalism so broadly that they can claim it is inevitable for planners.[6]

But I do not wish to quibble here about the proper use of "paternalism." Let Sunstein and Thaler keep their terminology. I will focus instead on Sunstein and Thaler's arguments for their version of paternalism.

1 Cass R. Sunstein and Richard H. Thaler, Libertarian Paternalism Is Not an Oxymoron, 70*U. Chi. L. Rev.* 1159 (2003).

2 Sunstein and Thaler (note 1), 1165.

3 Joel Feinberg, *Harmless Wrongdoing*, 1988, xix.

4 John Stuart Mill, *On Liberty* (Everyman's Library edition), 1859, 73.

5 Sunstein and Thaler (note 1), 1162.

6 Sunstein and Thaler (note 1), 1164-65 (For my contrary view, *see* sec. 3 below.).

2. Libertarian Moments in Sunstein and Thaler's Proposals

It is somewhat surprising to me how libertarian Sunstein and Thaler's proposals are by contemporary political standards, at least in Japan. They are opposed to a law ordering drivers to wear seatbelts on pain of a substantial fine,[7] although such laws exist in several European nations and a similar law causes little or no protest in Japan. Drivers in Japan are required not only to wear seatbelts themselves, but also to ensure that other persons in their cars do so as well. True, offenders are not fined. But a driver's repeated failure to wear a seatbelt leads to forfeiture of his or her driver's license. More importantly, Sunstein and Thaler do not endorse compulsory national health care schemes or universal pensions, both of which are backbones of welfare states and were introduced in Japan nearly half a century ago. In general, Sunstein and Thaler encourage planners, both public and private, to influence people for their own good, but they do not deny people freedom of choice. For example, Sunstein and Thaler propose legalizing a retirement pension plan with sufficiently high savings rate from which employees are free to opt out. It should be also noted that Sunstein and Thaler seem not to pay any attention to distributive concerns in their arguments.

I agree with many of Sunstein and Thaler's proposals concerning public policy. I have already written that their "libertarian paternalism" is not paternalistic in my sense. The influence of a planner on people by such means as default rules, framing and outright suggestions does not infringe people's freedom by itself. As a libertarian, I understand freedom in the good old sense of negative freedom: the absence of external coercion, not of influence. Libertarianism does not force people to make active choices. It leaves people free to be dependent or servile as well as to be autonomous. Thus, Sunstein and Thaler's proposals of libertarian paternalism seem as compatible with people's freedom as advertising, social pressure and contracts of adhesion, which critics of free markets usually consider detrimental to freedom.

Indeed, default rules, as well as contracts of adhesion, are not only compatible with freedom of choice, but are also often beneficial to the actors in that they give people regularity and reasonable expectations in their dealings and reduce transaction costs. Much of the value of contract law derives from its formulation of default rules. By contrast, family law chiefly consists of mandatory rules. I doubt the need for many of those rules and welcome Sunstein and Thaler's proposals on privatizing marriage as well as improving school choices in their recent book *Nudge*.[8]

7 Sunstein and Thaler (note 1), 1186.

8 Richard H. Thaler and Cass R. Sunstein, *Nudge*, 2008, chs. 13 + 15.

3. When Even Soft Paternalism Is Not Permissible

But, it does not necessarily follow that I agree wholly with their position. First, it is not always permissible for the government to influence people for their alleged welfare without coercion. Suppose the government acknowledges freedom of religion, but takes one religion, say Christianity, as the default rule and requires non-Christian students to seek permission to be absent without penalty from Christian religious classes in public schools. Even though this scheme might be justifiable for pragmatic reasons in an overwhelmingly Christian society and compatible with freedom of religion, no libertarians or liberals would find it acceptable, because it is blatantly against the separation of religion and state. But neither libertarians nor liberals are opposed to Christian religious instruction in private schools. The difference between their attitudes to public and private schools is based not on the degree of religious influence on students, but rather on the fact too little appreciated by Sunstein and Thaler that public schools are run by governments and financed through taxation, whereas private schools are not. Thus, Thomas Jefferson famously wrote in *Virginia Statute of Religious Freedom,* 1779:

> To compel a man to furnish contributions of money for the propagation of opinions which he disbelieves and abhor is sinful and tyrannical.

Reasons for the government's neutrality in matters of world views such as religion and moral beliefs are not limited to individual freedom. Law and other public systems have an important function even without any exercise of coercion. They have a symbolic or expressive function of authoritatively denouncing some activities and recommending some others, and they do it at the expense of public money, i.e. taxes. As is often the case, the best approach for governments to take towards such controversial and/or delicate matters as religion is to do nothing and adopt a *laissez-faire* attitude. Not only strong paternalism, but also weak paternalism as proposed by Sunstein and Thaler, is to be avoided in these realms. Governmental paternalism is *not* at all inevitable and neutrality is required here. Libertarians are opposed to governmental activity itself here as well as paternalism, not because personal freedom is thereby infringed (it is possible that it is not), but because it is simply not the government's business in the first place.

I think that consideration applies not only to such solemn matters as religion, but also more mundane activities such as eating and smoking, where Sunstein and Thaler propose libertarian paternalism. Indeed, taste in food and drink matters more than religion for many people. Sunstein and Thaler do not seem to be very sensitive to diversity between different persons' values there. True, long life and good health are valued by almost all human beings, but there are many other important things besides them. The palatal pleasure of some sinful foods may be more valuable to *bon vivants* than a new lease of life. Similar things can be said of other people whose lifestyle is not conducive to a long and healthy life. Public planners should hesitate to discourage people from taking part in supposedly unhealthy habits or risky activities.

In *Nudge,* Sunstein and Thaler spend a couple of pages on the requirement of governmental neutrality.[9] There, they admit "a form of neutrality is sometimes both feasible and important"[10] in such case as ballot design and free exercise of religion. But, they also claim nudges (the choice architecture of libertarian paternalism) are desirable when the Nudger is likely to be able to help the Nudgee make a better choice. I am less sanguine in general of the government's ability to nudge and the propriety of public decision concerning the matters of personal life.

4. When Allegedly Irrational Behavior Can Be Rational

Secondly, I suspect Sunstein and Thaler exaggerate people's practical irrationality or, to put it more mildly, bounded rationality. It must be admitted that orthodox economics tends to presuppose that economic actors are perfectly rational, fully informed, autonomous and stable. Recent behavioral economics reveals the unreality of such *homo economicus* models. But, I am of the opinion that some behavioral patterns often considered irrational can be rational. Although rationality is, admittedly, a controversial concept,[11] I hope to show how some kinds of allegedly irrational behavior can be rational in an everyday sense. It should be kept in mind that the concept of rationality in the context of libertarian paternalism is evaluative and is not used to make predictions concerning human actions.

First, I do not find anything irrational by itself in time preference and time discounting as I find nothing irrational in the preference for self-interest over other people's interests.[12] Since myself in the near future is more closely connected with me now than my distant future self is, my interests in the near future are, from my present viewpoint, more important than those in the distant future. Here, I personally subscribe to Derek Parfit's claim that what matters in survival is not personal identity *per se*, but rather psychological relations between selves of different times.[13] However, I hasten to add that I do not mean caring for one's distant future or other people to the same degree as for one's present self is necessarily irrational. Such patterns of care can be rational, too. It is quite possible that there is not a single rational course of action, but many rational courses which are incompatible with each other. What I claim is merely that time preference can be as rational as both self-interested behavior and altruism.

9 Thaler and Sunstein (note 8), 246-48.
10 Thaler and Sunstein (note 8), 246.
11 *See*, e. g., Robert Nozick, *The Nature of Rationality,* 1993.
12 cf. Sunstein and Thaler (note 1), 1168.
13 Parfit, *Reasons and Persons,* 1984, Part III.

I also wish to point out that such things as commitment and sense of duty play substantial roles in human actions even if they do not contribute to the interest of the agent, or anyone else for that matter. An agent may feel obligated to perform some act by a certain code. Such behavior may well be irrational from a consequentialist perspective, but it can be rational or even mandatory from a deontological viewpoint. This consideration may partly explain the notoriously irrational behavior of taking into consideration sunk costs. Anyway, even if some desires were irrational as means to an end, their satisfaction may bring genuine pleasure to the actor. Connectedly, some attitudes such as overconfidence are irrational in epistemological terms but not necessarily so in practical terms. We are sometimes encouraged by optimism to unlikely achievement. Overconfidence in oneself can be more beneficial in practice than unbiased assessment.

Next, preferences and desires are things that a particular person has in a particular concrete condition. When we take into account this consideration, endowment effects need not be a sign of irrationality, because it is an obvious fact that many people feel strongly attached with what they possess. And, since every person and condition is different in some respects and a human being changes over time, it is only natural that human preferences are not stable. Unstableness of preferences does not mean the lack of freedom or rationality on the part of an actor.

Finally, although many people are less informed about general relevant facts in their own decisions than are other knowledgeable people, including public planners, the latter must be much more ignorant of people's individual values and preferences (which even those individuals often cannot articulate, but which they reveal by their behavior in real concrete situations).

My remarks in this section are not intended to show that real people are always rational, but they do suggest that Sunstein and Thaler overestimate their practical irrationality.

5. Conclusion

While I sympathize with much of Sunstein and Thaler's libertarian paternalism, I have some misgivings about their case, as I have discussed above. But I am sure of one great merit of their argument: it makes us appreciate the importance and justifiability of many kinds of governmental actions which influence people for their own welfare without apparent coercion, such as default rules and framing.

Susumu Morimura
Department of Law
Hitotsubashi University
Tokyo, Japan

Itaru Shimazu, Chiba, Japan

We, John Jones, Choose

Comment on Cass R. Sunstein & Richard H. Thaler, Libertarian Paternalism is Not an Oxymoron, 70 *U. Chi. L. Rev.* 1159 (2003)

John Jones, a character Sunstein is describing in his *Free Markets and Social Justice*, is a perfect model of myself. Mr. Jones does and says various things which contradict each other: "He is in favor of mandatory recycling not withstanding his own failure to recycle."[1]

One of Sunstein's main points was to emphasize the importance of social norms as the background against which people choose. The economists' favored idea of "revealed preference" places heavier stress on what people really do, not recycling in this case, than on what they say or think; i.e. "We should recycle." But, since people can join their collective decisions to constitute at least some part of the social norms, they achieve a sort of autonomy if they can succeed in doing what they think they should by forcing themselves by means of a new rule, which would punish non-recyclers in this case. I would call this idea *collectivized Kantianism* in which man's sense of norms prevails over their *akrasia* or weak will. The most problematic word here is, of course, "collectivized," which might ruin the whole idea of "autonomy" and make Kant himself indignant.

While in the book, *Free Markets and Social Justice,* he tried to support people in collective decisions [who choose] to behave morally, in his paper on *Libertarian Paternalism,*[2] and the book, *Nudge,*[3] he is proposing another device with which to support weak individuals in their personal decision making.

When I wrote a short essay on the "evolutional theory of contract" I came up with a similar idea and emphasized the default rule in contract law. The world in which perfect freedom of contract applies might be dangerous for us with limited information, experience, calculating ability, and weak determination. So, I argued that judges must have wider discretion in judging whether a new type of contract, which is claimed to be the result of freedom of contract by one party in a lawsuit, is reasonable and viable as an addition to the list of typical contracts. But, in his *Libertarian Paternalism* Sunstein is extending the idea of default rules beyond the traditional field of typical contracts and applying it in the general field where some decision making by the agent is required but where we cannot expect the agent to be capable of good decisions.

1 Cass R. Sunstein, *Free Markets and Social Justice*, 1999, 34.
2 Cass R. Sunstein & Richard H. Thaler, Libertarian Paternalism is Not an Oxymoron, 70 *U. Chi. L. Rev.* 1159 (2003).
3 Richard H. Thaler and Cass R. Sunstein, *Nudge: Improving Decisions About Health, Wealth, and Happiness*, 2008.

I almost totally agree with him in his criticism of the economic man model which appears in standard text books of economics. Since I have found that his argument is utilizing the recent achievements of behavioral economics, I even started reading the literature in this field.

I also found that Sunstein's argument helps me in dealing with the problems like that of requiring motorcycle riders to wear helmets. While it seems obviously intuitive that such coercion must be permitted, I have been finding it difficult within the present arena or our legal and moral discussion to argue for it. The defense of such a measure of minor paternalism by referring to the third party's interest, e.g. that of the potential defendants in a tort case, seems to be too roundabout or farfetched. The solution I think he is giving for paternalism is that under the circumstance of bounded rationality and bounded self control, it is sometimes better for people to get support for their decision-making through paternalistic regulations in some sort. If I had read his book 20 years ago, I could have written a better paper on paternalism than I actually did.

In short, I do not think the phrase "libertarian paternalism" is an oxymoron. But, I have some questions to ask. To save time, I enumerate my questions;

1. What is the difference between libertarian paternalism and "soft paternalism" which has been a popular solution in this area? Or, what can libertarian paternalism do which soft paternalism cannot?
2. From a Hayekian point of view, the most powerful device with which people cope with the problems of decision making in the market is "competition as a discovery procedure." Usually, competition is defended for productive efficiency, but competition is as important in the field of consumption. Consumers also have to learn somehow to be wise consumers. In competition, various solutions are tried in the market first, and after some successful solutions are found and many pioneers have lost in their adventure, people just imitate the success. In this view, market is a collective trial and error mechanism the purpose of which is to cope with our innate limit of information. I find in Sunstein's paper little discussion on this point, i.e. the Austrian School's explanation of the market, which is different from the standard explanation of mainstream economics. This fact may reveal the difference between him and Hayek in the understanding of the market system. Consequently, he seems to have a more pessimistic idea on the market than Hayek.

   Obviously, the most problematic part in his theory has to do with the "planner" which appears here and there in his paper. Although he (or she) is not the planner of the planned economy pretending omniscience, he still carries something more than the name to share with his notorious ancestor. Although the planner is supposed to be more intelligent than the regular person, he cannot know in advance what he does not know. And, the best solution might be in the area that he does not yet know.

So, I believe there must be some device to make competition possible within Sunstein's model of the planner.

The solution might be sought in the idea of profession. Professionals are well informed and experienced while having varying ideas among themselves concerning what might be the right answer for the matter in question. So, competition and open arguments among experts may be a promising direction to look for the alternative for bureaucrats as planners.

3. If we limit the scope of our policy with which to intervene in people's individual choices by libertarian paternalism, there is no possibility at all of introducing redistribution. In countries committed to the idea of the welfare state, e.g. Germany and Japan, systems of medical care, pension, education, etc, are run in order to both support individual decision making and to organize some sort of redistribution among the rich and the poor.

   If these systems were to be transformed into being run by libertarian paternalism, which allows an opportunity for the unsatisfied to opt out, it would be impossible to continue the redistribution because most of the rich who are taxed heavily will be likely to opt out of the system. This will surely cause trouble with egalitarians.

   I assume Sunstein has some framework other than those run in the spirit of libertarian paternalism to achieve his version of social redistribution. Then, whatever that may be, it will become the main battle field between him and hard core libertarians. That means the main problem concerning his libertarian paternalism is not in the idea itself, which is reasonable enough, but in the question how thoroughly he is going to apply it. I believe that, the wider the range is, i.e. the less the room is in which he is ready to resort to other more coercive measures, the better our world will be.

Itaru Shimazu
Chiba University
Chiba, Japan

Kazumasa Inaba,[1] Nagoya, Japan

Sunstein's Theory for Modern Administrative State: A Potential of Republican Model of Judicial Review.

Comment on Cass R. Sunstein, Beyond Judicial Minimalism, in: *Judicial Minimalism: For and Against,* Ninth Kobe Lecture, Aoyama Gakuin University, Tokyo, Japan, June 7, 2008.

This paper comments on Professor Cass Sunstein's theory of the judicial review of administrative actions. The question I am concerned with is the logical relationship between the administrative or regulatory process and judicial review. In brief, we can imagine two models of statutory interpretation: a court-centered model and an agency-centered model. This is a hard question of administrative law: *See* the recent case, *Massachusetts v. EPA*, 549 U.S. 497 (2007). From the point of view of an administrative law scholar in Japan, this essay evaluates whether Professor Sunstein's analysis has a universal application across social, economical and legal differences in modern countries. His argument seems to limit the scope of review of administrative actions while pursuing deliberation in the administrative process for several public values. His logic is very interesting when contrasted with the effort of the Japanese government, which started administrative reforms in the 1980s and then has tried to expand the role of judicial review through its Justice System Reform agenda since the 1990s.[2]

Before we discuss the judicial review theory of Professor Sunstein, it will be useful to address his understanding of *Chevron, Inc. v. NRDC*, 467 U.S. 837 (1984). The reason we will examine this case is that, as many public law scholars point out, the theory of judicial deference has been a major issue in United States administrative law circles since the U.S. Supreme Court adopted a "two step" approach in *Chevron*. Professor Sunstein is known as one of the proponents of Hard Look reviews into the U.S. public law study; therefore, he would criticize *Chevron* if it adopted a weak and narrow scope of judicial review.[3] However, at first, he explains *Chevron* step 1 as an expression of the "non-delegation canon," that is the notion in his thinking that "basic value judgments should be made by Congress."[4]

1 My appreciation to IVR Japan who gave me the chance to write this comment and Professor Yasutomo Morigiwa for his generous advice.

2 *See, e.g., Recommendations of the Justice System Reform Council* (2001), http://www.kantei.go.jp/foreign/policy/sihou/singikai/990612_e.html.

3 Cass R. Sunstein, Interest Groups in American Public Law, 38 *Stanf. L. Rev.* 29, 60-61(1985) ("The most important doctrinal innovation in administrative law, for example, is the hard-look doctrine.").

4 Cass R. Sunstein, Changing Conceptions of Administration, 1987 *B. Y. U. L. Rev.* 927, 941.

Next, concerning *Chevron* step 2, Professor Sunstein argues that the judicial deference adopted in *Chevron* means deference to the deliberation by administrative agencies, and he tries to set limits on the range of *Chevron* in subsequent cases.[5] In my understanding, he proposes a kind of synthetic theory of administrative process and judicial review for statutory interpretation in modern administrative states.

I think Professor Sunstein can show us two important problems concerning the limits of judicial review. The first problem relates to the political ideology of judicial review in U.S. He argues in his articles that several Judges in famous cases were not free from the policies adopted by the Presidents who appointed them.[6] Therefore, fundamental value judgments should be considered not by the court but by Congress or the President. His argument for judicial minimalism seems to be peculiar to the U.S. context; it would not always be applicable to situations in other countries, including Japan.

The second problem, and the more important one, is the logical relationship between the regulatory process and judicial review. Professor Sunstein's argument is known as one of civic republicanism; attempting to justify an agency's positive role in fostering deliberation. According to him,

> The principal virtue of technical knowledge is that it informs regulatory decisions by <u>shedding light on their potential effects</u>...the role of the administrator is not merely to reflect constituent pressures or to aggregate private interests. Instead, the purpose of <u>the regulatory process is to select and implement the values that underlie the governing statute and that, in the absence of statutory guidance</u>, must be found <u>through a process of deliberation</u>[7]

While his proposal might be distinguished in the U.S. because the U.S. Constitution does not adopt the notion of administrative power, unlike Germany or Japan, it is very interesting for Japanese administrative law scholars that civic republicans, including Professor Sunstein, propose the public legitimacy of administrators and judicial deference to their deliberative process in the U.S., which has a tradition of strong judicial review. Especially when we consider contemporary administrative law problems such as the cost and benefit of human rights protection in social welfare or environmental protection, I find his argument to be adequate across different social structures in many countries.

In contrast to the validity of his argument for judicial minimalism or deference for administrative deliberation, several questions remain. We encounter dif-

5 Cass R. Sunstein, Chevron Step Zero, 92 *Va. L. Rev.* 187, 225 (2006). In reality, the Court indicated such an expression in *United States v. Mead Corp.*, 533 U.S. 218, 230 (2001). "It is fair to assume generally that Congress contemplates administrative action with the effect of law when it provides for a relatively formal administrative procedure tending to foster the fairness and deliberation that should underlie a pronouncement of such force."

6 Cass R. Sunstein, Testing Minimalism: A Reply, 104 Mich. L. Rev. 123, 128 (2005); Thomas J. Miles and Cass R. Sunstein, The Real World of Arbitrariness Review, 75 *U. Chi. L. Rev.* 761 (2008).

7 Cass R. Sunstein, Factions, Self-Interest, and the APA: Four Lessons since 1946, 72 *Va. L. Rev.* 271, 281-82 (1986)(emphasis added).

ficulties when we consider a global social economic trend such as the New Public Management, aiming for market-like efficient and reduced governmental organizations after the 1980s. Does the democratic deliberative process mean a costly and time-consuming process, as encouraging meaningful participation and changing original preferences is a difficult task for many administrative agencies?

I have no problems with administrative agencies fostering public deliberation, but if conditions capable of fostering deliberation are lacking, it would be an impracticable idea. Otherwise, public deliberation would be a negotiated deal process between several groups having a big voice[8]. In order to reduce the problems, it is not enough to state that the deliberative process deserves a kind of judicial minimalism or deference. Alternatively, it could be argued that the deliberative process should be accompanied by reforms such as government re-organization and increases in specialized and experienced government regulation.

Hence, the major unanswered question in arguments of Professor Sunstein would be the conditions under which his judicial review model can work in practice. This is not an easy question. His argument on judicial minimalism or deference offers an objective analysis of the current state of judicial review of administrative actions in the U.S. and, as noted above, his theory is a good argument about how we think in relation to preserving judicial review while justifying technical knowledge of administrators to solve modern complex and difficult problems.

Turning back to the Japanese situation, I feel compelled to describe the reason why the theories of judicial deference and legitimacy of administrative power were not discussed fully in Japan. In Japanese society, as many scholars have pointed out, judicial review of administrative actions was not extensive and rigorous, even in the post war period. Many public law scholars were cautious about some kinds of judicial deference that could weaken the role of judicial power for human rights protection. Such unique social conditions in Japan seemed to prevent the theoretical and practical advancement of a legal system in which administrative power and judicial power each have their own [or inherent] role for the task of human rights protection.

Therefore, given the Japanese social structure, judicial minimalism in which courts should review whether agencies decided deliberatively or not has the potential to be a valid theory, but it depends on the possibility of structural change in which administrative agencies foster public deliberation by legal reforms such as enacting laws to expand civic participation and by non-legal developments from civil servants to recover the people's trust in them and their public administration. Even in a globalizing era, when we consider the historical diversity of

8 One problem would be the "tractability" as pointed by Prof. Coglianese. See Eric Orts & Cary Coglianese, Collaborative Environmental Law: Pro and Con, 156 *U. Pa. L. Rev.* PENNnumbra 289, 297 (2007).

court and administrations interdependencies in different countries, we find different conditions which equally justify the minimization of judicial review.

Kazumasa Inaba
Graduate School of Law
Nagoya University
Nagoya, Japan

Reply

Cass R. Sunstein

On Fallibility: A Reply

Any account of legal interpretation, of constitutional law, or of government regulation must come to terms with the problem of human fallibility.

We can identify three dimensions of fallibility. The first is *simple ignorance*. Judges, constitution-makers, citizens, and regulators often lack relevant knowledge. They do not know what the future will bring. The second problem involves reliance on *heuristics* – mental shortcuts or rules of thumb. Often these heuristics work well, but they can lead to serious and systematic errors. For example, people assess risks by asking whether relevant events are cognitively "available," in the sense that they can easily be brought to mind. Use of the "availability heuristic" can produce major mistakes. The third problem involves *biases*. Both individuals and organizations show such biases. For example, people tend to care about fairness, but their judgments about fairness are self-serving. Interest-group pressures and simple self-interest can lead both citizens and representatives to behave in a biased fashion.

Along with many others, I have been interested in three apparently unrelated projects, involving minimalism, deliberative democracy, and libertarian paternalism. At first glance, these projects do indeed seem unrelated, but there is an important connection: Each of them involves human fallibility. Minimalist judges favor small steps. They know that they do not know. Their knowledge of their own ignorance moves them toward narrow, shallow decisions. Minimalists avoid visionary decisions, in the form of wide rulings and theoretical ambition, precisely because they believe that such decisions may go badly wrong.

For their part, deliberative democrats are skeptical not only of tyrants, but also of populists who claim to speak for democratic ideal. Deliberative democrats want to combine reflection and reason-giving with a degree of accountability. They know that ignorance of fact, heuristics, and biases can lead the public in unfortunate directions. They favor deliberation as a check on potential blunders.

Libertarian paternalists respect freedom of choice, but they insist that choosers often go badly wrong.[1] They emphasize that ignorance, heuristics, and biases can lead people to endanger their health and their livelihood; they want public officials to provide some help. They want to use "choice architecture" to nudge people in better directions. In this way, libertarian paternalists object to those who invoke the "rational actor" model to suggest that people's decisions will promote their welfare. They believe that people are boundedly rational, and that they are inevitably influenced by subtle features of the environment. Libertarian paternal-

1 See Richard H. Thaler and Cass R. Sunstein, *Nudge*, 2008.

ism want those features to be designed in a way that will help people rather than hurt them.

At the same time, libertarian paternalists are entirely aware that such officials are hardly infallible. They are skeptical about aggressive mandates and bans, because they know that regulators may themselves suffer from simple ignorance, and may use heuristics, and suffer from biases, that lead them in unfortunate directions. They believe that socialists, antidemocrats, and authoritarians of all kinds have paid far too little attention to the fallibility of government officials. They want to preserve freedom of choice in part as a safeguard against official errors. If officials blunder, freedom of choice can provide an indispensable safety valve.

Our principal topic here is jurisprudential, but I am grateful to the various commentators for helping to demonstrate the importance of a clear understanding of human fallibility to social thought in multiple domains. More generally, I am grateful to the commentators for offering numerous suggestions, clarifications, and corrections, and for raising questions and doubts about many of my arguments. I shall be thinking about their contributions for many years to come. Because of the number and detail of the comments, I think it would be useful here, not to engage them specifically or in sequence, but to attempt some general clarifications that will at least briefly engage with a number of their concerns. I know that my response will be inadequate and I express my apologies as well as my gratitude for their many excellent points.

As several of the commentators show, minimalism is not an approach for all times and all seasons. In some contexts, narrowness leaves a great deal of unpredictability; people need to know what the law is. In other contexts, shallowness is not possible. Sometimes a decision cannot be made without a degree of theoretical ambition. In fact one of the main goals of my Kobe Lecture is to elaborate the foundations of minimalism while also identifying the contexts in which judges should, or must, move in more ambitious directions.

As Yasuo Hasebe suggests, we can indeed have an incompletely theorized agreement on behalf of incompletely theorized agreements. Some people will accept shallowness for purely pragmatic reasons; perhaps judges will be unable to agree on a deep ruling. Other people will accept shallowness on the ground that judges lack information; perhaps deep rulings will turn out to be wrong. Still other people may accept shallowness because of a belief in mutual respect. Perhaps it is most respectful to attempt to preserve and accommodate, rather than to reject, the defining commitments of other people; Yoh Matsuo offers a valuable discussion here. Narrowness might similarly be defended by those with a wide range of starting points. Hirohide Takikawa offers a superb discussion of some of the possible grounds for minimalism, and what he says is an important improvement on my own account.

In my view, the arguments for and against minimalism are not limited to any particular nation. A number of the comments, including Takehiro Ohya's, ask whether the arguments apply to career judges; I believe that they do. There is no reason why career judges might not choose to rule narrowly and shallowly. On the other hand, it is true that in some situations, judges have enough information and experience to be more ambitious, and a major goal of the Kobe Lecture is to identify these situations. It is also true that in circumstances of great transition, the argument for minimalism is simultaneously strengthened. In the midst of transition, large steps, from the judiciary, might turn out to be insufficiently informed, because the future is unpredictable. But in the midst of transition, major departures from past practices might well be justified; consider the case of South Africa. I therefore agree with Makoto Usami that judges sometimes should and even must ask some deeper questions. And it is true that institutional differences, especially in the domain of judicial review, can affect the appeal of various doctrines (see the valuable comments of Kazumasa Inaba).

It is important to see that minimalists do not necessarily defer to the democratic process; they do not adopt a strong presumption in favor of whatever the legislature decides. Those who believe in a consistent policy of judicial restraint, or who favor respect for whatever legislatures do, are not minimalists in the sense that I understand them here. Consider in this regard the remarks of Hidetomi Omori, who perhaps misunderstands me on this point, and Yoh Matsuo, who asks whether minimalists favor popular constitutionalism; they do not. Minimalists are willing to strike down the outcomes of legislative processes. The key point is that when they do so, they seek to rule narrowly and shallowly.

Let me turn, in this light, to the question of libertarian paternalism. My basic hope is that on many questions that engage contemporary governments, diverse people might be able to converge on an approach that combines freedom of choice with a gentle nudge. In the domain of environmental protection, for example, we might be able to do a great deal without coercion; the same is true in domains involving health, savings, and investments.[2] It is true, to be sure, that those who favor redistribution from rich to poor will favor mandates, above all through the tax system, rather than nudges (see Itaru Shimazu's comment). If we want to give large sums of money to the poor, we will probably have to use the tax system to coerce wealthy people to help. But many nudges will assist those at the bottom of the economic ladder; help for those who need it is a principal interest of libertarian paternalists.

Susumu Morimura does raise some excellent questions about the meaning and limitations of libertarian paternalism. I would like to focus here on his claims about the issue of government neutrality. It is true that if we care about such neutrality, some nudges will be impermissible. In a free and democratic society, the government should not be allowed to nudge people into accepting a certain set of religious convictions, or into voting for a particular political candidate, or into speaking out against certain political ideas. Different nations differ on the details,

2 For many examples, see id.

but democracies agree that in certain domains, neutrality is required. We might even be able to accept an incompletely theorized agreement in favor of government neutrality. With respect to religion, for example, neutrality can be justified on numerous and diverse grounds (see the relevant remarks of Hirohide Takikawa).

But I am not sure that Susumu Morimura is right to suggest that the requirement of neutrality applies to other domains, such as eating and smoking. Must government really be neutral as between smoking and not smoking? As between healthy eating and unhealthy eating? As between obesity and normal weight? To be sure, mandates and bans should be disfavored. Free people have a right to eat a lot of ice cream, even if ice cream is fattening, and libertarian paternalists do not want to ban smoking. But in many domains, people's decisions reflect their own fallibility, and where human fallibility leads to bad outcomes, a gentle, noncoercive intervention can do a great deal of good.

Consider, for example, governmentally-mandated disclosure policies, which should be adopted in many domains. From the standpoint of the right account of neutrality, is there a valid objection to compulsory disclosure of the risks associated with smoking? In my view, disclosure requirements should be applied far more generally. In fact such requirements might have done a great deal to help prevent future financial crises of the sort that beset the United States in 2008.

I do not deny that in some cases, it is necessary to make controversial claims in order to resolve disputes over the legitimacy of paternalistic measures, even those that preserve freedom of choice. In the United States, an evident example involves abortion: Is it permissible for government to try to nudge women to carry their children to term? Reasonable people disagree. Other nations will be able to identify their own examples. In general, the minimalist strategy is both simple and attractive: *To the extent possible, we should attempt to bracket our deepest differences and to see if we can decide what to do, even as we are uncertain, or disagree, about why, exactly, we ought to do it.* In my view, the minimalist strategy usually works well as a defense of libertarian paternalism.

A final point by way of conclusion. I have suggested, with several of the commentators, that incompletely theorized agreements can be defended on multiple grounds. In the end, however, one of those grounds seems to me the most powerful. It involves respect.

In both private and public life, people's fundamental convictions may seem to be at stake, and one or another approach might repudiate the defining beliefs of one or another group. In some cases, judges and others are explicitly asked to take sides. Of course it is true that in prominent cases, it is crucial to take sides – against Communism, against Nazism, against terrorism, against torture, against racial discrimination, against sex discrimination, against disability discrimination, against discrimination on the basis of sexual orientation. But in many cases, reasonable people differ, and in such cases, it is important for human beings, including judges, to acknowledge their own fallibility. One of America's greatest judges, Learned Hand, once said that "the spirit of liberty is that spirit which is not too sure that it is right." An acknowledgement of fallibility, central to minimalism, is a way of respecting liberty's spirit; and it carries with it a strong signal of mutual respect.

Notes on the Contributors

Cass R. SUNSTEIN, the 9th Kobe Lecturer, is the Felix Frankfurter Professor of Law at Harvard Law School. He is now on leave to serve in the Obama Administration as the Administrator of the White House Office of Information and Regulatory Affairs. His recent publications include *A Constitution of Many Minds: Why the Founding Document Doesn't Mean What It Meant Before*, Princeton University Press, 2009, *Going to Extremes: How Like Minds Unite and Divide, Oxford University Press*, 2009, *Nudge: Improving Decisions about Health, Wealth, and Happiness* (co-author with Richard Thaler), Yale University Press, 2008.

HASEBE Yasuo is Professor of Constitutional Law at School of Law, University of Tokyo. He published numerous articles including "August Revolution Thesis and the Making of the Constitution of Japan", *Rechtstheorie,* Beiheft 17 (1997), "Constitutional Borrowing and Political Theory", *International Journal of Constitutional Law*, vol.1, No.2 (2003), and "The Rule of Law and Its Predicament", *Ratio Juris*, Vol.17, No.4 (2004). He can be contacted at hasebe@j.u-tokyo.ac.jp

INABA Kazumasa is Associate Professor of Administrative Law at the Graduate School of Law, Nagoya University. He is the author of *Housougyousei No Houkouzou To Kadai* (or Legal Structure of Contemporary Broadcast Administration), Nipponhyoronsha, 2004, and also of articles including "Jouhoukoukaihousei No Tekiyoutaishouhoujin No Kakudai (or A Study on Public Access Law that should be Applied to Corporations Exercising Administrative Powers in Japan)", *Nagoya University Journal of Law and Politics*, vol.225, 2008. He can be contacted at inaba@law.nagoya-u.ac.jp

KAMEMOTO Hiroshi is Professor of Jurisprudence at the Graduate School of Law, Kyoto University. He is the author of *Hōtetsugaku* (or *Philosophy of Law*), Seibundo, Tokyo, 2011 and *Hoteki Shiko* (or *Legal Thinking*), Yuhikaku, Tokyo, 2006.

MATSUO Yoh is Lecturer of Legal Philosophy at the Faculty of Law, Kinki University. He is the author of following articles. Hōkaishakuhōhōron Niokeru Seidorontekitenkai: Kinji no America Kenpōkaishakuhōhōron wo Sozaitoshite (Institutional Turn in Theory of Legal Interpretation: One Dimention of Recent Developments in Theory of Constitutional Interpretation in America), *Minshōhōzasshi* vol.140 no.1 and no.2 (2009) and Architecture niyoru Kiseisayo no Seishitsu to Sono Igi (Natures of Regulatory Functions in Architecture and its Significance), *Hōtetsugaku Nenpō* 2007 (2008). He can be contacted at y_matsuo@jus.kindai.ac.jp

MORIGIWA Yasutomo is Professor of Jurisprudence at the Graduate School of Law, Nagoya University. He is the editor of *Hōsō no Rinri* (or *Ethica Juris Peritorum*), Nagoya University Press, 2nd ed. 2011, *Tisiki toiu Kankyo* (or *The Environment Called Knowledge*), Nagoya University Press, 1996, and author of numerous articles including "The Semantic Sting in Jurisprudence; H. L. A. Hart's Theories of Language and Law," *ARSP*, Beiheft, vol. 40, 1991. He can be contacted at morigiwa@nagoya-u.jp

MORIMURA Susumu is Professor of Law at the Graduate School of Law, Hitotsubashi University. His research interests include libertarianism, personal identity, property and human rights, and Locke. He is the author of five books, all in Japanese, including *Jiyu wa Dokomade Kanoka* (*How Much Freedom Is Possible?*), Kodansha, 2001, and *Zaisanken no Riron* (*A Theory of Property Rights*) Kobundo, 1995, and many papers including "The Libertarian View of Human Nature", *ARSP*, Beiheft Nr. 107, 2007. He can be contacted at morimura.susumu@r.hit-u.ac.jp

OHYA Takehiro is Associate Professor of Philosophy of Law at the Graduate School of Law, Nagoya University. He is the author of two books, *Hōkaishaku no gengo tetsugaku: kuripuki kara kongenteki kiyakushugi e* [*On Justifiability of Legal Interpretation: from Kripke to Radical Conventionalism*], Keisō Shobō, 2006, and *Jiyū towa nanika: kanshi shakai to "kojin" no shōmetsu* [*Person and its Liberty in the Information Age*], Chikuma Shobō, 2007. He also wrote several articles including "Relation between Surveillance and Liberty: Difference of restriction ex ante and ex post", *Keisatsugaku Ronshū* [*The Journal of Police Science*], August 2008. He can be contacted at t-ohya@law.nagoya-u.ac.jp

OMORI Hidetomi is Professor of Philosophy of Law at Graduate School of Humanities and Social Science, Okayama University. He is the author of a book named *Kyouwashugi No Houriron: Koushi Bunri Kara Shingiteki Democracy E* (or *A Republican Theory of Law: From Public/Private Separation to Deliberative Democracy*), Keisoushobou, 2006, and also of several articles including "Berlin No Jubaku Wo Koete: Jean-Fabien Spitz Niokeru Jiyuu No Gainen" (or Au delà de l'enchaînement de Berlin: sur la conception de liberté chez Jean-Fabien Spitz), *Okayama Law Journal* vol.57 2007. He can be contacted at omori@cc.okayama-u.ac.jp

SHIMAZU Itaru is Professor at the Law School, Chiba University. He is the author of *Jiseiteki Chitsujo* (or *The Spontaneous Order*), Bokutakusha Pub. Co., 1985, and articles including "The Individual and Collective Decisions; Concepts of Law and Social Change", Law and Justice in a Global Society, IVR 2005, Granada, *anales de la catedra francisco suarez* no.39, 2005, "Legal Mind as Basic Faculty for the Citizens of Liberal States", *ARSP*, Beiheft Nr. 97, "Captives of Ideas; Old and New", Chiba Law Review, 2005, "Who is to Suffer from Misfortune", *University of*

Hawai'i Law Review, vol.15, 1993, "Spontaneity and Peace", *Asia University Law Review* vol.21-2, 1987. He can be contacted at Itaru@faculty.chiba-u.jp

TAKIKAWA Hirohide is Professor of Philosophy of Law at Rikkyo University. He is the author of a book titled *Sekinin no Imi to Seido* (or *The Significance of Responsibility*), Keisoshobo, 2003, and numerous articles including "Can We Justify the Welfare State in an Age of Globalization? Toward Complex Borders", *ARSP*, Vol.92, Heft.1, 2006 and "Conceptual Analysis of Accountability: The Structure of Accountability in the Process of Responsibility" in *Envisioning Reform: Enhancing UN Accountability in the Twenty-first Century*, edited by Sumihiro Kuyama and Michael Ross Fowler, United Nations University Press, 2009. He is the winner of IVR Young Scholar's Prize 2005. He can be reached at tkkw71@gmail.com

USAMI Makoto is Professor of Law and Philosophy at the Tokyo Institute of Technology. He is the author of three books and over forty journal articles and book chapters, including "Law as Public Policy: Combining Justice with Interest," in Tadeusz Biernat and Marek Zirk-Sadowski (eds.), *Politics of Law and Legal Policy* (Wolters Kluwer Polska, 2008), "Global Justice: Redistribution, Reparation, and Reformation," *ARSP*, Beiheft 109 (2007), and "Retroactive Justice: Trials for Human Rights Violations under a Prior Regime," in Burton M. Leiser and Tom D. Campbell (eds.), *Human Rights in Philosophy and Practice* (Ashgate, 2001). He can be contacted at usami@soc.titech.ac.jp

ARCHIV FÜR RECHTS- UND SOZIALPHILOSOPHIE – BEIHEFTE

Herausgeben von der Internationalen Vereinigung für Rechts- und Sozialphilosophie (IVR).
Die Bände 1–4 sind im Luchterhand-Fachverlag erschienen.

Franz Steiner Verlag ISSN 0341-079X

76. Kurt Seelmann (Hg.)
Kommunitarismus versus Liberalismus / Communautarisme contre Libéralisme / Communitarismo verso Liberalismo
Vorträge der Tagung der Schweizer Sektion der Internationalen Vereinigung für Rechts- und Sozialphilosophie vom 23.–24. Oktober 1998 in Basel
2000. 163 S., kt.
ISBN 978-3-515-07657-9

77. Kurt Seelmann (Hg.)
Nietzsche und das Recht / Nietzsche et le Droit / Nietzsche e il Diritto
Vorträge der Tagung der Schweizer Sektion der Internationalen Vereinigung für Rechts- und Sozialphilosophie vom 9.–12. April 1999 in Basel
2001. 270 S., kt.
ISBN 978-3-515-07745-3

78. Alexander Bröstl / Marijan Pavcnik (Hg.)
Human Rights, Minority Rights, Women's Rights
Proceedings of the 19th World Congress of the International Association for Philosophy of Law and Social Philosophy in New York, 24th–30th June 1999
2001. 145 S., kt.
ISBN 978-3-515-07861-0

79. Michael Anderheiden / Stefan Huster / Stephan Kirste (Hg.)
Globalisierung als Problem von Gerechtigkeit und Steuerungsfähigkeit des Rechts
Vorträge der 8. Tagung des Jungen Forum Rechtsphilosophie vom 20.–21. September 2000 in Heidelberg
2001. 170 S., kt.
ISBN 978-3-515-07870-2

80. Elspeth Attwooll / Annette Brockmöller (Hg.)
Applied Ethics at the Turn of the Millenium
Proceedings of the 19th World Congress of the International Association for Philosophy of Law and Social Philosophy in New York, 24th–30th June 1999
2001. 122 S., kt.
ISBN 978-3-515-07903-7

81. Kurt Seelmann (Hg.)
Wirtschaftsethik und Recht
Vorträge der Tagung der Schweizer Sektion der Internationalen Vereinigung für Rechts- und Sozialphilosophie im Oktober 2000 in Fribourg/Schweiz
2001. 123 S., kt.
ISBN 978-3-515-07899-3

82. Michel Troper / Annalisa Verza (Hg.)
Legal Philosophy: General Aspects
Concepts, Rights and Doctrines. Proceedings of the 19th World Congress of the International Association for Philosophy of Law and Social Philosophy in New York, 24th–30th June 1999
2002. 208 S., kt.
ISBN 978-3-515-08026-2

83. Gralf-Peter Calliess / Matthias Mahlmann (Hg.)
Der Staat der Zukunft
Vorträge der 9. Tagung des Jungen Forum Rechtsphilosophie in der Internationalen Vereinigung für Rechts- und Sozialphilosophie vom 27.–29. April 2001 an der Freien Universität Berlin
2002. 226 S., kt.
ISBN 978-3-515-08048-4

84. Winfried Brugger / Görg Haverkate (Hg.)
Grenzen als Thema der Rechts- und Sozialphilosophie
Referate der Tagung der Deutschen Sektion der Internationalen Vereinigung für Rechts- und Sozialphilosophie vom 22.–23. September 2000 in Heidelberg
2002. 218 S., kt.
ISBN 978-3-515-08042-2

85. Paricia Smith / Paolo Comanducci (Hg.)
Legal Philosophy: General Aspects
Theoretical Examinations and Practical Application. Proceedings of the 19th World Congress of the International Association for Philosophy of Law and Social Philosophy in New York, 24th–30th June 1999
2002. 176 S., kt.
ISBN 978-3-515-08100-9

86. Hirokazu Kawaguchi / Kurt Seelmann (Hg.)
Rechtliche und ethische Fragen der Transplantationstechnologie in einem interkulturellen Vergleich
2003. 180 S., kt.
ISBN 978-3-515-08132-0

87. Rolf Gröschner / Gerhard Haney (Hg.)
Die Bedeutung P. J. A. Feuerbachs (1755–1833) für die Gegenwart
Tagung der Deutschen Sektion der Internationalen Vereinigung für Rechts- und Sozialphilosophie vom 15.–16. März 2002 in Jena
2003. 240 S., kt.
ISBN 978-3-515-08193-1

88. Arend Soeteman (Hg.)
Pluralism and Law I
Justice. Proceedings of the 20th World Congress of the International Association for Philosophy of Law and Social Philosophy in Amsterdam, 2001
2003. 203 S., kt.
ISBN 978-3-515-08327-0

89. Arend Soeteman (Hg.)
Pluralism and Law II
State, Nation, Community, Civil Society. Proceedings of the 20th World Congress of the International Association for Philosophy of Law and Social Philosophy in Amsterdam, 2001
2003. 193 S., kt.
ISBN 978-3-515-08362-1

90. Arend Soeteman (Hg.)
Pluralism and Law III
Global Problems. Proceedings of the 20th World Congress of the International Association for Philosophy of Law and Social Philosophy in Amsterdam, 2001
2004. 217 S., kt.
ISBN 978-3-515-08446-8

91. Arend Soeteman (Hg.)
Pluralism and Law IV
Legal Reasoning. Proceedings of the 20th World Congress of the International Association for Philosophy of Law and Social Philosophy in Amsterdam, 2001
2004. 195 S., kt.
ISBN 978-3-515-08503-8

92. Christian Hiebaum / Peter Koller (Hg.)
Politische Ziele und juristische Argumentation
Symposium der Internationalen Vereinigung für Rechts- und Sozialphilosophie vom 11.–12. Oktober 2002 in Graz
2003. 142 S., kt.
ISBN 978-3-515-08284-6

93. Jan C. Joerden / Roland Wittmann (Hg.)
Recht und Politik
Jahrestagung der Deutschen Sektion der Internationalen Vereinigung für Rechts- und Sozialphilosophie vom 26.–29. September 2002 in Frankfurt an der Oder
2004. 184 S., kt.
ISBN 978-3-515-08458-1

94. Philippe Mastronardi (Hg.)
Das Recht im Spannungsfeld utilitaristischer und deontologischer Ehtik
Vorträge der Tagung der Schweizer Sektion der Internationalen Vereinigung für Rechts- und Sozialphilosophie vom 15.–16. November 2002 in Luzern
2004. 170 S., kt.
ISBN 978-3-515-08366-9

95. Aleksander Peczenik (Hg.)
Justice
Proceedings of the 21st World Congress of the International Association for Philosophy of Law and Social Philosophy in Lund (Sweden), 12th–18th August 2003
Volume 1
2004. 218 S., kt.
ISBN 978-3-515-08483-3

96. Yasutomo Morigiwa / Fumihiko Ishiyama / Tetsu Sakurai (Hg.)
Universal Minority Rights?
A Transnatioal Approach. Proceedings of the 5th Kobe Lectures. Tokyo and Kyoto, December 1998
2004. 126 S., kt.
ISBN 978-3-515-08504-5

97. Svein Eng (Hg.)
Law and Practice
Proceedings of the 21st World Congress of the International Association for Philosophy of Law and Social Philosophy in Lund (Sweden), 12th–18th August 2003
Volume 2
2005. 213 S., kt.
ISBN 978-3-515-08524-3

98. Kenneth Einar Himma (Hg.)
Law, Morality, and Legal Positivism
Proceedings of the 21st World Congress of the International Association for Philosophy of Law and Social Philosophy in Lund (Sweden), 12th–18th August 2003
Volume 3
2004. 183 S., kt.
ISBN 978-3-515-08513-7

99. Günther Kreuzbauer / Silvia Augeneder (Hg.)
Der Juristische Streit
Recht zwischen Rhetorik, Argumentation und Dogmatik
2004. 166 S., kt.
ISBN 978-3-515-08480-2

100. Ulfrid Neumann / Winfried Hassemer / Ulrich Schroth (Hg.)
Verantwortetes Recht
Die Rechtsphilosophie Arthur Kaufmanns. Tagung vom 10.–11. Mai 2003 in München
2005. 188 S., kt.
ISBN 978-3-515-08580-9

101. Kurt Seelmann (Hg.)
Menschenwürde als Rechtsbegriff
Tagung der Schweizer Sektion der Internationalen Vereinigung für Rechts- und Sozialphilosophie vom 25.–28. Juni 2003 in Basel
2004. 175 S., kt.
ISBN 978-3-515-08591-5

102. Zenon Bankowski (Hg.)
Epistemology and Ontology
Proceedings of the 21st World Congress of the International Association for Philosophy of Law and Social Philosophy in Lund (Sweden), 12th–18th August 2003
Volume 4
2005. 195 S., kt.
ISBN 978-3-515-08707-0

103. Carsten Bäcker / Stefan Baufeld (Hg.)
Objektivität und Flexibilität im Recht
Tagungen des Jungen Forums Rechtsphilosophie in der Internationalen Vereinigung für Rechts- und Sozialphilosophie im September 2004 in Kiel und im April 2005 in Hagen
2005. 213 S., kt.
ISBN 978-3-515-08743-8

104. Robert Alexy (Hg.)
Juristische Grundlagenforschung
Tagung der Deutschen Sektion der Internationalen Vereinigung für Rechts- und Sozialphilosophie vom 23.–25. September 2004 in Kiel
2005. 251 S., kt.
ISBN 978-3-515-08640-0

105. Philippe Mastronardi / Denis Taubert (Hg.)
Staats- und Verfassungstheorie im Spannungsfeld der Disziplinen
Tagung der Schweizerischen Vereinigung für Rechts- und Sozialphilosophie vom 12.–13. November 2004 an der Universität St. Gallen
2006. 255 S., kt.
ISBN 978-3-515-08851-0

106. José Juan Moreso (Hg.)
Legal Theory / Teoría del derecho
Legal Positivism and Conceptual Analysis / Positivismo juridico y análisis conceptual. Proceedings of the 22nd World Congress of the International Association for Philosophy of Law and Social Philosophy in Granada, 2005
Volume 1
2007. 263 S., kt.
ISBN 978-3-515-08910-4

107. José Rubio Carrecedo (Hg.)
Political Philosophy / Filosofía política
New Proposals for New Questions / Nuevas propuestas para nuevas cuestiones. Proceedings of the 22nd World Congress of the International Association for Philosophy of Law and Social Philosophy in Granada, 2005
Volume 2
2007. 239 S., kt.
ISBN 978-3-515-08911-1

108. Andrés Ollero (Hg.)
Human Rights and Ethics / Derechos humanos y Ética
Proceedings of the 22nd World Congress of the International Association for Philosophy of Law and Social Philosophy in Granada, 2005
Volume 3
2007. 323 S., kt.
ISBN 978-3-515-08912-8

109. Nicolás López Calera (Hg.)
Globalization, Law and Economy / Globalización, Derecho y Economía
Proceedings of the 22nd World Congress of the International Association for Philosophy of Law and Social Philosophy in Granada, 2005
Volume 4
2007. 321 S., kt
ISBN 978-3-515-08913-5

110. Josep Aguiló-Regla (Hg.)
Logic, Argumentation and Interpretation / Lógica, Argumentación e Interpretación
Proceedings of the 22nd World Congress of the International Association for Philosophy of Law and Social Philosophy in Granada, 2005
Volume 5

2007. 206 S., kt.
ISBN 978-3-515-08914-2

111. Marcel Senn / Dániel Puskás (Hg.)
Gehirnforschung und rechtliche Verantwortung
Fachtagung der Scheizerischen Vereinigung für Rechts- und Sozialphilosophie vom 19.–20. Mai 2006 an der Universität Bern
2006. 171 S., kt.
ISBN 978-3-515-08963-0

112. Annette Brockmöller (Hg.)
Hundert Jahre Archiv für Rechts- und Sozialphilosophie (1907–2007)
Auswahl 14 bedeutender Aufsätze von Kelsen, Radbruch, Luhmann u. a.
2007. 330 S., kt.
ISBN 978-3-515-09100-8

113. Horst Dreier / Eric Hilgendorf (Hg.)
Kulturelle Identität als Grund und Grenze des Rechts
Akten der Tagung der Internationalen Vereinigung für Rechts- und Sozialphilosophie vom 28.–30. September 2006 in Würzburg
2008. 374 S., geb.
ISBN 978-3-515-09101-5

114. Jochen Bung / Brian Valerius / Sascha Ziemann (Hg.)
Normativität und Rechtskritik
Tagungen des Jungen Forums Rechtsphilosophie in der Internationalen Vereinigung für Rechts- und Sozialphilosophie im September 2006 in Würzburg und im März 2007 in Frankfurt am Main
2007. 269 S., kt.
ISBN 978-3-515-09130-5

115. Marcel Senn / Dániel Puskás (Hg.)
Rechtswissenschaft als Kulturwissenschaft?
Kongress der Schweizerischen Vereinigung für Rechts- und Sozialphilosophie vom 15.–16. Juni 2007 an der Universität Zürich
2007. 220 S., kt.
ISBN 978-3-515-09149-7

116. Annette Brockmöller / Eric Hilgendorf (Hg.)
Rechtsphilosophie im 20. Jahrhundert
100 Jahre Archiv für Rechts- und Sozialphilosophie
2009. 207 S., kt.
ISBN 978-3-515-09285-2

117. Marcel Senn / Barbara Fritschi (Hg.)
Rechtswissenschaft und Hermeneutik
Kongress der Schweizerischen Vereinigung für Rechts- und Sozialphilosophie vom 16.–17. Mai 2008 an der Universität Zürich
2009. 258 S., kt.
ISBN 978-3-515-09155-8

118. Bart C. Labuschagne / Ari M. Solon (Hg.)
Religion and State
From separation to cooperation? Proceedings of the Special Workshop "Legal-philosophical reflections for a de-secularized world" held at the 23rd World Congress of the International Association for Philosophy of Law and Social Philosophy in Kraków, 2007
2009. 209 S., kt.
ISBN 978-3-515-09368-2

119. Martin Borowski (Hg.)
On the Nature of Legal Principles
Proceedings of the Special Workshop "The Principles Theory" held at the 23rd World Congress of the International Association for Philosophy of Law and Social Philosophy in Kraków, 2007
2010. 182 S., kt.
ISBN 978-3-515-09608-9

120. Friedrich Toepel (Hg.)
Free Will in Criminal Law and Procedure
Proceedings of the 23rd and 24th World Congress of the International Association for Philosophy of Law and Social Philosophy in Kraków, 2007, and in Beijing, 2009
2010. 122 S., kt.
ISBN 978-3-515-09320-0

121. Marcel Senn / Bénédict Winiger / Barbara Fritschi / Philippe Avramov (Hg.)
Recht und Globalisierung / Droit et Mondialisation
Kongress der Schweizerischen Vereinigung für Rechts- und Sozialphilosophie, 15.–16. Mai 2009, Universität Genf / Congrès de l'Association Suisse de Philosophie du Droit et de Philosophie Sociale, 15–16 mai 2009, Université de Genève
2010. 196 S., kt.
ISBN 978-3-515-09673-7

122. Imer B. Flores / Uygur Gülriz (Hg.)
Alternative Methods in the Education of Philosophy of Law and the Importance of Legal Philosophy in the Legal Education
Proceedings of the 23rd World Congress of the International Associaction for Philosophy of Law and Social Philosophy "Law and Legal Cultures in the 21st Century: Diversity and Unity" in Kraków, 2007

2010. 114 S., kt.
ISBN 978-3-515-09695-9

123. Sascha Ziemann
Archiv für Rechts- und Sozialphilosophie: Bibliographie und Dokumentation (1907–2009)
2010. 434 S., kt.
ISBN 978-3-515-09719-2

124. Jan-Reinard Sieckmann (Hg.)
Legal Reasoning: The Methods of Balancing
Proceedings of the Special Workshop "Legal Reasoning: The Methods of Balancing" held at the 24th World Congress of the International Association for Philosophy of Law and Social Philosophy (IVR), Beijing, 2009
2010. 205 S., kt.
ISBN 978-3-515-09723-9

125. Edward Schramm / Wibke Frey / Lorenz Kähler / Sabine Müller-Mall / Friederike Wapler (Hg.)
Konflikte im Recht – Recht der Konflikte
Tagungen des Jungen Forums Rechtsphilosophie in der Internationalen Vereinigung für Rechts- und Sozialphilosophie in Tübingen und Göttingen
2010. 308 S., kt.
ISBN 978-3-515-09729-1

126. Kristian Kühl (Hg.)
Zur Kompetenz der Rechtsphilosophie in Rechtsfragen
Tagung der Deutschen Sektion der Internationalen Vereinigung für Rechts- und Sozialphilosophie vom 24.–26. September 2008 in Tübingen
2011. 140 S., kt.
ISBN 978-3-515-09816-8

127. Stephan Kirste / Anne van Aaken / Michael Anderheiden / Pasquale Policastro (Hg.)
Interdisciplinary Research in Jurisprudence and Constitutionalism
2012. 267 S. mit 2 Abb. und 2 Tab., kt.
ISBN 978-3-515-09941-7

128. Stephan Ast / Julia Hänni / Klaus Mathis / Benno Zabel (Hg.)
Gleichheit und Universalität
Tagungen des Jungen Forums Rechtsphilosophie (JFR) in der Internationalen Vereinigung für Rechts- und Sozialphilosophie (IVR) im September 2010 in Halle (Saale) und im Februar 2011 in Luzern
2012. 315 S., kt.
ISBN 978-3-515-10067-0

129. Bénédict Winiger / Matthias Mahlmann / Philippe Avramov / Peter Gailhofer (Hg.)
Recht und Verantwortung / Droit et responsabilité
Kongress der Schweizerischen Vereinigung für Rechts- und Sozialphilosophie, 11.–12. Juni 2010, Universität Zürich / Congrès de l'Association Suisse de Philosophie du Droit et de Philosophie Sociale, 11–12 juin 2010, Université de Zurich
2012. 206 S. mit 6 Abb., kt.
ISBN 978-3-515-10066-3

130. Thomas Bustamante / Oche Onazi (Hg.)
Global Harmony and the Rule of Law
Proceedings of the 24th World Congress of the International Association for Philosophy of Law and Social Philosophy, Beijing, 2009. Vol. 1
2012. 133 S., kt.
ISBN 978-3-515-10081-6

131. Thomas Bustamante / Oche Onazi (Hg.)
Human Rights, Language and Law
Proceedings of the 24th World Congress of the International Association for Philosophy of Law and Social Philosophy, Beijing, 2009. Vol. 2
2012. 192 S., kt.
ISBN 978-3-515-10082-3

132. Yasutomo Morigiwa / Hirohide Takikawa (Hg.)
Judicial Minimalism – For and Against
Proceedings of the 9th Kobe Lectures. Tokyo, Nagoya, and Kyoto, June 2008
2012. 99 S., kt.
ISBN 978-3-515-10136-3

133. Thomas Bustamante / Carlos Bernal Pulido (Hg.)
On the Philosophy of Precedent
Proceedings of the 24th World Congress of the International Association for Philosophy of Law and Social Philosophy, Beijing, 2009
Volume 3
2012. 144 S., kt.
ISBN 978-3-515-10150-9

134. Matthias Kaufmann / Joachim Renzikowski (Hg.)
Zurechnung und Verantwortung
Tagung der Deutschen Sektion der Internationalen Vereinigung für Rechts- und Sozialphilosophie vom 22.–24. September 2010 in Halle (Saale)
2012. 184 S., kt.
ISBN 978-3-515-10180-6